About This Book

Why Is This Topic Important?

Simulations are the first fundamental change to education since the textbook. They bridge the gap between repeatable classrooms and "real" skills learned in apprenticeships and on the job. They also insert a layer of automation into the education model that actually *improves*, not degrades, the learning process. Yet the understanding of what a simulation consists of is scarily incomplete. People are excited by what the military does. They see the opportunity when their children play with computer games. But they also see the embarrassingly bad "edutainment" titles and "business simulations." This book connects the dots of what needs to go into simulations to take advantage of this unique educational genre.

What Can You Achieve with This Book?

After reading this book, you will understand the challenges, skill sets, time frames, and processes involved in building one of the first-ever "genuine" business simulations. You will also understand the value proposition of a simulation. This will help you to be a better consumer and builder of simulations. Understanding simulations will also give any instructor or producer of instructional material a better understanding of the strengths and weaknesses of the broader profession, as well as his or her role in it. Finally, you will understand the long-term resolution of the seven simulation paradoxes:

- Simulations cost millions to build, and yet must be financially accessible to the smallest companies.
- Simulations take years to develop, and yet must be responsive to instant changes in business conditions.
- Simulations are e-learning, yet they are completely different from e-learning.
- Simulation development is risky, and yet the results have to be predictable.
- Users have to learn how to use a simulation, yet every moment with a simulation has to be valuable.
- Simulations borrow heavily from computer games, and yet they are not like any computer game.
- Simulations have to be realistic, but selectively so.

How Is This Book Organized?

The story begins in Part One: The Simulation Way. You will learn some of the reasons why building this simulation was critical to the e-learning industry. Most people will realize for the first time how different (and more powerful) simulations are, compared with every learning technique and process that came before them. Part Two: Modeling Reality describes the building of the simulation. It moves from a discussion of the design principles that guided the work through the details of the simulation's components—the calculation model, the dialogue and physics systems, the artificial intelligence, and, of course, the sets and figures. These chapters will describe skill sets that have never previously been necessary for educational design, but soon will be critical. Part Three: Philosophical and Technical Realities dives deeper into the story. Here is how the team handles the interface, plus issues of gameplay, scoring, consumer evaluation, and marketing. Finally, in Part Four: The Way Ahead, the book synthesizes the issues that will continue to challenge simulation developers and users. Simulations are powerful, but are only part of a solution. Future educational simulation projects will have a unique and necessary role in changing the nature of both education and work.

About Pfeiffer

Pfeiffer serves the professional development and hands-on resource needs of training and human resource practitioners and gives them products to do their jobs better. We deliver proven ideas and solutions from experts in HR development and HR management, and we offer effective and customizable tools to improve workplace performance. From novice to seasoned professional, Pfeiffer is the source you can trust to make yourself and your organization more successful.

Essential Knowledge Pfeiffer produces insightful, practical, and comprehensive materials on topics that matter the most to training and HR professionals. Our Essential Knowledge resources translate the expertise of seasoned professionals into practical, how-to guidance on critical workplace issues and problems. These resources are supported by case studies, worksheets, and job aids and are frequently supplemented with CD-ROMs, websites, and other means of making the content easier to read, understand, and use.

Essential Tools Pfeiffer's Essential Tools resources save time and expense by offering proven, ready-to-use materials—including exercises, activities, games, instruments, and assessments—for use during a training or team-learning event. These resources are frequently offered in looseleaf or CD-ROM format to facilitate copying and customization of the material.

Pfeiffer also recognizes the remarkable power of new technologies in expanding the reach and effectiveness of training. While e-hype has often created whizbang solutions in search of a problem, we are dedicated to bringing convenience and enhancements to proven training solutions. All our e-tools comply with rigorous functionality standards. The most appropriate technology wrapped around essential content yields the perfect solution for today's on-the-go trainers and human resource professionals.

Essential resources for training and HR professionals

Simulations and the
Future of Learning

To Slater

Simulations and the Future of Learning

An Innovative (and Perhaps Revolutionary)
Approach to e-Learning

Clark Aldrich

A Wiley Imprint
www.pfeiffer.com

Library of Congress Cataloging-in-Publication Data

Aldrich, Clark
    Simulations and the future of learning: an innovative (and perhaps
    revolutionary) approach to e-learning / Clark Aldrich.
       p. cm.
    Includes bibliographical references and index.
    ISBN 0-7879-6962-1 (alk. paper)
     1. Education—Simulation methods. 2. Internet in education. 3.
    Instructional systems—Design. I. Title.
    LB1029.S53A43 2004
    371.33'4—dc21

                                    2003009008

Acquiring Editor: Lisa Shannon
Director of Development: Kathleen Dolan Davies
Developmental Editor: Leslie Stephen
Editor: Rebecca Taff
Senior Production Editor: Dawn Kilgore
Manufacturing Supervisor: Bill Matherly
Cover Design: Chris Wallace
Illustrations: Lotus Art

Printed in the United States of America

Printing 10   9   8   7   6   5   4   3   2   1

Contents

Foreword

One of my favorite books is Tracy Kidder's Pulitzer Prize-winning, *The Soul of a New Machine* (1981. Reprinted in 2000 by Back Bay Books). Kidder lived with the Data General development team that built the first 32-bit processor and told the story of both the process of building the computer and the dynamics of the team. It read like a novel, though every word was true. It had drama, humor, pathos and ran the gamut of every human emotion. Clark Aldrich's has achieved a similar effect in *Simulations and the Future of Learning*. His detailed and fascinating story of the massive effort associated with developing probably the first high-fidelity leadership simulation is practically riveting. I know it sounds ridiculous. . .but it's true.

On a higher level, Clark compels us to the conclusion that there is truly no other way to learn than through simulations. Having done that, he scares us into the realities and complexities of doing worthwhile non-trivial work. Yet his account—and the understanding of why simulations are so powerful at achieving deep knowledge and probable behavior change, does not preach at us. It makes the reader truly think about the current linear models for learning. It reveals why the kind of analysis necessary to understand the many and interrelated variables in a situation often require us to reconceptualize an entire process. And it humbles us when and if we dare to offer superficial criticism of these intense efforts. His analysis of gaming and how an entire world of game players will probably learn little in traditional environments results in the realization that we are on a collision path with the current generation when we attempt to teach them with lectures and trivial interactions and exercises.

These new learners are highly stimulated, used to complexity, will tolerate uncertainty and intensely study the variables, rules and relationships, and strategies until they "win": until they "learn." Just watch any nine-year-old reading Game Boy® Advanced strategy books that look like hieroglyphics to an adult.

The book is a metaphor for the kind of change necessary for universities and organizations to change their view of e-learning. Unless they do we are doomed to linear instruction punctuated with gratuitous media dominated by content experts who haven't a clue about what it takes to achieve deep learning and skill. Believe it or not, the book also made me laugh out loud. In addition, I learned more about leadership by reading about the simulation than I have in thirty-five years of management training programs and book reading. These are serious accomplishments for what I expected to be a technical book.

July 2003   Gloria Gery

Acknowledgments

This book would not have been possible without:

My wife, Lisa;

The Virtual Leader Team: David Alloza, Marcus Burden, Graham Courtney, Olivier Gaudino, Jean-Michel Herve, Patrice Krysztofiak, Ken Kupersmith, Karim Osman, Tom Parkinson, Will Riley, and Pierre-Henri Thiault; and

Leadership exemplars Tim Ellis and Wayland Hicks.

Simulations and the Future of Learning

Chapter One

Do You Want Fries
with that e-Learning?

We believe there is enormous potential for e-learning
companies that can provide corporations with the
knowledge they need to compete effectively in the global
marketplace.
　　—*Michael T. Moe, Henry Blodget,* The Knowledge Web,
　　　　　　　　Merrill Lynch & Co., 23 May 2000

What would the world be like if e-learning truly worked? What if
you could experience something looking at your computer screen,
no matter where you were, that would give you more control over
your job and life and a deeper understanding of your world?

What would the world be like if that were the way e-learning
worked today?

Well, the training people in an organization would be more
powerful than the lawyers. Managers and employees would spend
considerable time plotting the next skill and experience sets they
needed to internally develop.

Schools would have class sizes of five, not twenty-five. Students
could actually engage with a teacher, as opposed to being on the receiving end of a lecture aimed at the "average" student. And they
would spend more of their time formally learning from one another
and from people all over the world.

Education would be a multi-billion dollar annual export. A
few countries would develop regional core competencies around
e-learning, much as countries have core competencies around cars
or wine. The financial impact would be on top of the revenue from
students who would still travel worldwide to our best universities.

1

And e-learning would produce buzz. There would be lots of advertising. The release of a new course would be a big deal. You would see people engrossed in it on their laptops next to you on the airplane, at the workplace, or across campuses.

The world would be like when the movie *Amadeus* came out—suddenly, an entire culture knew about Mozart. When a new e-learning course came out, suddenly everyone would be able to gain a working knowledge of some relevant skill. Schools would become repositories of great educational products. Adults would envy children for their school experiences.

And if the current vision of e-learning worked today, everyone who was willing to pay for it would have access, through the Web, to best practices, relevant news, simulations, performance tools for just-in-time learning, role models, mentors, experts, coaches, and fellow learners. Content would be customized by our interest and our proposed career paths. The world would be a learning community.

Everything would be controlled by a great uber-learning infrastructure, perhaps best visualized by Pensare (Figure 1.1). Learners would access everything through a giant portal that used industry standard, plug in content, serving it to them in a way that met their learning style.

Figure 1.1 Pensare's Vision of a Learning Community

A Long Time Coming, a Long Way to Go

That is not the case today. Not by a long shot.

Pensare is no longer in business. Training and education *have* been in an intense period of change over the last ten years. That is indisputable.

But in many ways we are further from the big goal than when we began. In so many ways e-learning has been evolving in the wrong direction entirely. In fact, so far, e-learning has made about the same contributions to learning as fast food has made to food.

Consider the basic similarities:

- The point of food is to nourish our bodies.
- The goal of learning in any organization (business, educational, governmental) should be to make its members more productive.

For decades, the fast-food industry has ignored the health needs of its consumers. The shaping forces for all of the burger and chicken restaurants have been industry driven. The food has become consistent across towns, states, and increasingly countries. Restaurant design is modular, with a set number of configurations that can fit into different environments. Menu entries must be easy to consume, never requiring utensils. Fast-food chains are constantly driving down the time you have to wait. There is pressure on every item to be low-cost and high profit.

e-Learning has been similarly focused on many factors besides increasing productivity. The shaping forces have come from a dotcom mentality. Content has to be streamed over the Web. It has to be designed for the least powerful machines in a corporation, connected with the thinnest Internet connections. And of course, there is the pressure for content to be low cost and high profit.

The core offerings of fast food today are hamburgers, chicken, and French fries. The core offerings of e-learning today are virtual classrooms and online workbooks (a.k.a. asynchronous e-learning).

Both e-learning and fast food have changed the role of the entrepreneur. The franchise model, used by McDonald's and other restaurant chains, increased a corporation's influence on the greatest number of people with the least risk. By giving up most of their freedom, local franchisees could add their hard work to established processes, run a successful business, and drive out local restaurants through increased productivity.

Likewise, in the late 1980s, a proliferation of toolkits gave masses of instructors more power to offer e-learning in exchange for more restrictions on its structure and function. (In 1985 IBM launched an authoring system for interactive videodisc. In 1986, Apple introduced HyperCard, an icon-based authoring system, for its Macintosh operating system, making it easy for everyone to create low-end e-learning. Soon after, Authorware and Toolbook were released.) All of these tools gave instructors the ability to reach significantly more people if they were willing to follow a highly structured, unforgiving process.

In the fast-food business, the rapid evolution of freezing, warehousing, and transportation technologies profoundly changed what we ate. Restaurant chains learned that they could mass-produce food at giant factories, sacrificing flavor and nutrition. Distributing those frozen burgers, buns, and fries ensured both a higher profit margin and a more consistent product than having local workers prepare fresh food near where it would be consumed.

Remarkably similarly, the proliferation of the Internet and Internet access in the early 1990s changed how employees learned. The content vendors learned that by taking out animated content, including video and most sound, they could more cheaply distribute content to more people at less cost. These vendors gave enterprises the ability to deliver a "course" anywhere in the world at any time.

Of course, this automation and scalability required strict processes and dedicated tools. The kitchens in fast-food chains became increasingly complicated and expensive to operate. They allowed fewer and fewer deviations from established rules, ultimately permitting only one way of doing anything. They required highly standardized inputs and outputs.

Learning management systems (LMSs) took this role in e-learning. They have become increasingly complicated and expensive to implement. LMSs allow fewer and fewer deviations from established rules. They absolutely require highly standardized inputs and outputs. Standards like SCORM and AICC require specific coding and criteria for interfacing with LMSs. ADL groups are working on standards for the instructional design of the content as well.

Meanwhile, the University of Phoenix has become the dominant e-learning university. It became clear to many that the Harvards and Whartons of the world, like the Four Seasons, would not be huge players in this new, ultra-competitive model.

Positioning was all-important. Kentucky Fried Chicken changed its name to KFC when the word "fried" assumed negative connotations in the marketplace. Similarly, several years later in 1999, CBT Systems, wanting to distance itself from its CD-ROM past, changed its name to SmartForce.

Unlike the fast-food industry's love affair with mass production and distribution technologies, the e-learning industry's faith in the Internet actually overshot in the late 1990s. In 1999, Knowledge-Planet launched and Asymetrix renamed itself Click2Learn.com to push e-learning portals as one-stop application service provider (ASP) models. Meanwhile the founders of Ninth House, launched in 1999, believed that widely accessible broadband would bring television-like e-learning to the masses. All three organizations had to back away from their aggressive plans within twelve months.

Drive-Through Content

Under that noise, a more sustainable short-term revolution was occurring. Just as drive-through windows revolutionized fast food, letting consumers quickly pick up a cola and a burger, or maybe just a cup of coffee, a new class of tools called learning content management systems (LCMS) emerged to change the face of e-learning. While they did not improve the quality of content (which had been steadily degrading for years), they made it easier to pick up just what was needed, when it was needed.

These LCMS authoring platforms gave learning organizations and vendors the ability to parse courses into smaller and smaller pieces, starting the industry down a path that would eventually break down many of the barriers between the disciplines of e-learning and knowledge management.

The changes continued to come at a faster rate.

Consolidation between vendors for efficiencies of scale became inevitable. KFC, Taco Bell, and Pizza Hut came together as a legal entity and increasingly began co-locating and branding. Smart-Force and SkillSoft merged in 2002, quickly eliminating their redundant staffs.

There are other similarities as well. Both industries continue to spend a huge portion of every revenue dollar on marketing, for example. Technology continues to be a double-edged sword. Grocery stores sell microwaveable frozen meals that provide people with alternatives to leaving their house or office to eat. So too have tools outside of the e-learning industry such as Instant Messenger and Microsoft Messenger begun to provide cheaper and more convenient alternatives to what some vendors offer.

The number of similarities between the fast-food chains and e-learning is staggering. But there is a huge difference. McDonald's (and Burger King and Wendy's and Carl's Jr.) market to and sell directly to the person who eats the burger. They at least have to care about the short-term flavor.

But few e-learning vendors dare sell their wares directly to the end-learner. Amazon does not carry a single e-learning course. Vendors would rather sell to the HR person, who will probably never even taste the stuff. The challenge here is self-evident: Making content appealing to the end-learner may be the lesson that the e-learning industry needs to learn most of all.

Who Cares the Most?

Across the decades, it seems bizarre that incredible amounts of technology and investment have actually made e-learning content progressively worse. But all you have to do is look up the nutritional information on your favorite fast-food restaurant's chicken nugget see how it can happen (and know that it is true).

Against a decade of dot-coming education, however, new, substantially better models of computer-based education have quietly emerged. They are forcing learning in a new direction. Take computer games, for instance.

Who hasn't watched a computer game and thought about education? As we watch our kids play a game, or get into one ourselves, thoughts like these go through all of our heads:

- Look at how much is going on.
- Look at how fluidly he or she has (or I have) learned how to use this.
- There has got to be some substantial learning going on.
- Why does all of this seem so vacuous? Who cares about shooting villains or racing a car?
- There has to be an opportunity here. What if there were valuable content presented this way?
- Why can't learning be more like this?

This range of reactions might be dismissed as mere intellectual flights of fancy, a rebellion against the stacks of textbooks and manuals that we have read and yet never really learned anything from. However, there are examples with more gravitas that lead us further down the same path.

Learning in Organizations That Care

What organizations would you say care the most about training? What organizations have no margin of error—as in, if their employees are not trained, people die?

Right, airlines training pilots and the military training soldiers. The United States military may be the greatest training organization of all time. And what learning method do they most rely on? You guessed it: simulations. Why? Because, as Al Sciarretta of CNS Technologies describes it for the military, "[W]e can no longer train for a very focused operation, e.g., military operations in Europe against the very conventional force of the USSR."

This is a continuation of Al's quote.

Nowadays, the military must be very flexible; being able to train for attaining "capability" levels that can be used against many conventional and unconventional threats rather than for opposing a specific threat. Thus, the importance of training readiness has increased significantly over the last decade. Costs, force size reduction, the need for realism, and other factors have driven the need for and use of simulation-based training as a substitute for live training at all levels of the training experience.

They have one criterion for using simulations: Does the new skill matter? If you are the military preparing soldiers, you will do a simulation first.

And if you are an airline training a pilot, you will use a simulation before you involve real passengers. If you are teaching someone how to handle a nuclear power station, you will use a simulation. If you are Wall Street training someone to handle millions of dollars, you will use a simulation.

In short, the observation is straightforward. *The organizations that care the most about training use simulations* to do their training and development heavy lifting.

The Mandate: Do It Differently or Do Not Do It at All

Meanwhile, vice presidents in all types of organizations are increasingly asking the training groups to evaluate all of their programs. The message is: Do them effectively or do not do them at all.

And employees, including managers, who need to deal with complicated situations, and the under thirty-five crowd, who grew up on computer games, are increasingly asking the training groups to "give me something to which I can relate."

The interactive capabilities of computers continue to relentlessly leap ahead. Every six months a new generation of graphic card is announced.

People learn by doing. They want to practice skills repeatedly in safe environments until they are well-honed, understanding their roles and the roles of the larger systems around them.

Simulations are coming of age. And this book shows you why and how to look at and understand simulations to help you become an effective consumer, deployer, user, or producer.

A Simulation Story

This book tells the story of conceiving, designing, building, and marketing a new-generation educational simulation. It makes the most of the ingredients I believe are necessary for success:

- Authentic and relevant scenarios;
- Applied pressure situations that tap users' emotions and force them to act;
- A sense of unrestricted options; and
- Replayability.

As you vicariously experience the making of that simulation, you will not just better understand the nuts and bolts decisions and activities driving such an undertaking but also develop deeper insight to the promise and pitfalls of the emerging world of e-learning.

The story begins in Part One: The Simulation Way. You will learn some of the reasons why my colleagues and I realized that building this sim was critical to the e-learning industry. The story line begins to lay out the basic questions and issues we grappled with, some philosophical, many nitty-gritty, all common to any future simulation design. Most people will realize for the first time how different (and more powerful) simulations are compared to every learning technique and process that came before them.

Part Two: Modeling Reality takes the story into actually building the sim. It moves from a discussion of the design principles that guided our work through a description of the details of the sim's components—the calculation model, the dialogue and physics systems, the artificial intelligence, and, of course, the sets and figures. These chapters will introduce skill sets that have never previously been necessary for educational design, but soon will be critical. Feel free to skim any of the four technical "systems" chapters: The Animation System, The Dialogue System, The Physics System, or The AI System.

Part Three: Philosophical and Technical Realities dives deeper into the story. Here is how we handled the interface plus issues of game play, scoring, consumer evaluation, and marketing.

Finally, in Part Four: The Way Ahead, I have attempted to synthesize from our experience the questions that I believe will continue to plague simulation developers and users. I make the argument that this and future educational simulation projects will have a unique and necessary role in changing the nature of both education and, ultimately, work itself.

Part One

The Simulation Way

Chapter Two

In the Game

Unlike the scripted, paper-driven exercises of
the past, computer simulation has become a must.
In fact, it may be the only way to represent the
complexities of future warfare.
—*Lieutenant General Eugene D. Santarelli,*
Vice Commander, Pacific Air Forces, USAF,
Air Component Support to Joint Exercises

There's a joke I heard a while back. There is a small village, known across the country for their food and their mountains—and for their monthly lottery. The local school raffled quilts to raise money.

One of the villagers, a woman named Greta, worked tirelessly for the poor. She made clothes and bread for the needy. She gave away every penny she ever earned.

The thing she wanted most in the world was to win the lottery. It started off as whim. She thought how much better she would sleep with a nice quilt. Then it grew into an obsession. But month after month, year after year, she never won. And she grew bitter. She still did her work, but resentfully. She was often heard muttering angrily to herself as she delivered food. Every night before going to bed, looking at her shabby bed, she moaned up to the heavens, "I am your humble servant. I do everything I believe you want. All I ask is one thing. I just want to win the lottery once. Is that so much?"

One night, a booming voice came down from the heavens. "Greta!"

"Yes," she said, trembling.

"Buy a ticket!"

If You Want to Understand Simulations, Play a Computer Game First

If you want to understand simulations, the only way to do it is to become familiar with today's computer games. Games are not educational simulations, of course. But they can introduce you to many of the structures, standards, and techniques built into simulations today. Understanding computer games is your ticket to win the lottery.

(By the way, solitaire doesn't count. And it also doesn't count if you only watch someone else play a computer game; it may even count against you! You have to go through all of the experiences first-hand.)

You will not always be impressed with what you experience, especially at first. Even the best games are terrible if judged by the linear standards set by television and movies. Computer games are typically full of blocky animation, clumsy dialogue, obvious production flaws, and melodramatic scripts.

You will get past this.

You will see that they actually redefine scalable experiences, adding breathtaking interactivity, and can convey extraordinary amounts of content. There is a reason why computer games are a $10 billion business today, and growing.

For anyone who develops educational content, or modifies it, or purchases it, or teaches to it, or has a stake in his or her organization's learning strategy for long-term business results, understanding the interactivity and production values of a modern computer game experience is critical.

If you aim too far below current games, you risk both boring your audience and missing out on effective ways to teach new types of skills. But if you aim too high above that mark (perfection or bust), you will either spend huge amounts of resources without any return at all or use that as an excuse to waddle on the sidelines.

It is easy to know whether you need to brush up your experience with this new medium. If your computer has the W-A-S-D keys worn down, or you wake up in the middle of the night with a new strategy to play, feel free to skip this. You are already ready. But if you are shocked at the violence in Grand Theft Auto® III based on the clips shown on network news, or if you still think of computer games in terms of how goofy people look when they are playing them, you have some work to do.

The first step is to make sure your computer is up to snuff. To play a current computer game, you will need a top-of-the-line computer circa turn of the century, namely a Pentium III (at least 300MHz), 32MB RAM, sound card, and a 3D accelerated graphics card or a Macintosh 2000 or later with OS 9.X or the newer OS X. If you do not have one, see if you have a friend who does. If none of your friends do, make new friends. Worst case, buy a new computer. It is the future of your organization—not to mention your career—we are talking about.

Microsoft's Midtown Madness

Start your education with one of Microsoft's Midtown Madness® games, preferably Midtown Madness® 2. It is a highly accessible game, with a very shallow learning curve. Choose the free-drive mode, and pick a car.

Figure 2.1 Cover of Midtown Madness® 2

Box shot reprinted with permission from Microsoft Corporation.

You will find yourself on the roadways of a major city. There is nothing you *have* to do. There are no time limits or goals. This is just to play. Drive around. Drive on the road. Drive off the road. You will smash into the cars ahead of you. Get yelled at by pedestrians. You will lose control and sideswipe a bus. You will deliberately accelerate when a drawbridge is going up to see if you can jump it.

Try following the traffic rules. Try breaking the rules. You will often get away with it if you do. This game is not politically correct. Try driving a few different vehicles, including the smallest car and the largest truck.

When you are ready to move on, note what parts of the Midtown Madness experience are realistic and what parts are not. Also notice what aspects of driving reality are captured well, for example, the mass of the vehicle with regard to steering, speed, and jumping. Also identify what aspects are not captured, such as fuel consumption.

You can drive seemingly anywhere in Midtown Madness, even into shop windows. But to get in the habit of observing what makes a game tick, also look for the boundaries of Midtown Madness as you play. They use water, buildings, and rotaries cleverly to keep you from going in one direction, say north, indefinitely.

While not a perfect game, Midtown Madness is a great first exposure to computer games. It epitomizes a sense of experimentation, playing off of our own "real-world" experience. It will be entertaining and worth playing for about an hour.

RollerCoaster Tycoon®

Next, try RollerCoaster Tycoon® (or, again, the ever-so-slightly better sequel, RollerCoaster Tycoon 2®). In this game, you try to develop land into a successful theme park. You can place rides and paths anywhere you want. You can set prices. You can manage your staff. You have to meet the needs of hundreds of simulated customers.

Figure 2.2 Cover of RollerCoaster Tycoon 2®

RollerCoaster Tycoon2® courtesy of Atari Interactive. © 2003 Atari Interactive, Inc. All Rights Reserved. Used with Permission.

Go to any of the starting scenarios. Log in a few hours of playing, and then spend a few minutes sizing up the experience.

The first hour with any new computer game (or, for advanced players, a new computer game genre) is pretty confusing. You don't know what you are doing. You make huge mistakes. Things are happening on the screen for no obvious reason. You want to do something simple, but you don't know how. Or you are constantly being told why you can't do things. The interface seems twitchy and oversensitive. The experience seems blocky, rough, and off-putting. It is like learning a new operating system.

Then things start to make sense. You are in the zone. In RollerCoaster Tycoon, you actually feel like the builder of an amusement park. You start to worry about customers. They need change; they need new experiences. You get excited when your research team has produced a new ride. You start playing with admission prices. You hire some full-time mechanics to make sure your equipment is running smoothly.

After you are comfortable with the interface and the game play, try to win some of the early scenarios. Try to build an amusement park that brings in a certain number of customers at a certain satisfaction level. You will probably not do it the first few iterations.

And I predict you will feel frustrated. When you do, walk away. Do something else. Come back in a few hours and try again. Or sleep on it. In most cases, when you try again, you will succeed. That's good. Frustration, and then getting past it, is probably necessary for learning.

Soon relationships become obvious. It seems inconceivable that you didn't understand it the first time around. If you were a power gamer, you might go to a website where people swap strategies. Use Google to try and find one if you want.

If you build two or three parks, they will probably be more similar than not, that is, the modifications will be relatively minor. Now watch someone else play. He or she will build a park in ways that you never even considered. You know you are thinking too linearly if you keep trying to correct what the other person is doing!

You don't need to become a great Roller Coaster Tycoon player. Just win one of the easy scenarios, and it is time to move on.

The Sims™

The next game to install is The Sims™. Go through the mini-tutorial. Build a house. Buy things. See what happens.

A few aspects of The Sims will strike you almost immediately. The first is how incomplete and rudimentary the game seems. The Sims don't talk, they mumble. The situation doesn't feel realistic at all. A day goes by too quickly to accomplish everything you need to. Cleaning the house is a drag. The interface feels confusing and you have trouble figuring out what to do to make things happen.

The second thing to notice is how much fun it is. Earning money and improving the quality of your simulated life is extremely rewarding. You can decorate your house the way you always wanted to or experiment with furnishings that in real life have been ruled out by your inherent good taste. You can buy expensive toys like a huge plasma television. You can flirt shamelessly with your neigh-

Figure 2.3 Cover of The Sims™ Deluxe Edition

bor's spouse. You can sleep late and invite friends over instead of going to your job.

You will soon understand why The Sims is the bestselling computer game of all time. You may even be able to reflect a bit on your own life. Time is a precious commodity. There is never enough of it to do everything you want. Meeting multiple goals at the same time (such as comfort and entertainment) is necessary. Even articulating a set number of goals and trying to meet them is more than most of us successfully accomplish.

Beyond the Open End

Midtown Madness, RollerCoaster Tycoon, and The Sims are open-ended games. There is no story, save the one you make up around it.

To finish your early exposure to computer games, I would recommend you play one game that is linear (at least in a computer game sort of way). Pick a game where you play highly defined characters. These games are often from the genre First-Person Shooters, because the action takes place around, and from the perspective of, a consistent character that you control.

If you can stand the carnage, try a few hours of Max Payne™. This is a highly stylized, highly emotional experience. You will get to know the title character very well. You will know his voice, how he moves, and his motivation. You will witness cinematic "cut-scenes" that move the story along. You will find yourself in huge, meticulously crafted sets that would impress George Lucas.

If you want something lighter, try Star Trek Voyager™: Elite Forces. You will play an extended episode derived from the science-fiction television show. You will interact with computer versions (so-called avatars) of the main characters from the show. There are plot twists. You will take breaks between the action to get the background story. You will be surrounded by a well-defined supporting cast (newly created for the game) and overhear their conversations. If you don't protect them in a firefight, they will die.

If you can tolerate an experience that is dark, violent, and brooding, try Deus Ex™. This may be a perfect computer game. It both gives you a highly structured story and the ability to play it on your terms. If you want to evolve your character into a sneaky James Bond type, you can. If you want to evolve your character into a Terminator-like creature, you can. You can make a thousand decisions along the way to make your onscreen character reflect how you want to play the game. You can choose stealth over brute force. You can scavenge or you can buy. You have to prioritize which tools to bring along and which to leave behind. On top of that, most of the challenges can be solved in different ways as well. Deus Ex gives you a nearly open-ended environment that encourages you to be creative and rewards your deviousness.

Into the Simulation Age

Spending $100 on games and putting in five to ten (to twenty) hours to increase your own awareness of how they work and why is absolutely necessary to understand this book and understand educational simulations broadly. It will be hard. And it will be exhilarating. You have to be a student, and a pathological learner. Buy guides if you want, but do not use them instead of experiencing the game yourself.

There once were newspaper people who criticized television for being too superficial. There were railroad executives who disparaged airplanes as being too expensive. They rejected electronic journalism and air transportation because they were comfortable with their world. Playing a couple of computer games is not sufficient, of course, to get you out of your comfort zone and immediately involved in creating or championing simulations for your organization's e-learning arsenal. But it is the lottery ticket that you must buy if you want a chance to contribute in the future.

Chapter Three

The Primary Colors of Content

We have become focused not on how to identify
our own uniqueness, but on how to mimic the mark
and style of others. We have been told that if we
can look like others, act like others, indeed, argue
as others, perhaps then we can be successful. . . .
The great quest is to find the individual "soul-
print," the singular stamp that belongs only to us.
—*Gerry Spence,* How to Argue and Win
Every Time: At Home, at Work, in
Court, Everywhere, Every Day

As you played through Midtown Madness, Roller Coaster Tycoon, and The Sims, you probably noticed that they integrated different types of content. For the sake of simplification, let's call them *linear, cyclical,* and *open-ended.* As with primary colors, they are distinct content forms, but are most effective when they are combined seamlessly.

Linear Content

Linear content is the form with which most of us are familiar. Movies, television shows, and books are all linear. So are most speeches and lectures.

Modern DVDs represent the purist extension of linear content today. The quality of sound and video is extraordinarily high. They have some interactivity. A viewer can rewind, pause, or move freely between scenes or chapters. There can be tangents—excursions into new areas—with returns to the original track. Deleted scenes can be added.

There can be different paths through the content. There is even a type of hidden linear content—Easter eggs. Easter eggs (in this context) are pieces of content only available to those who are told or can figure out how to reach them. For example, a DVD may have a hidden archive of production art, available only if the viewer knows enough to click on a certain graphic at a certain time.

Here's one from www.dvdeastereggs.com: "For the DVD Sopranos Season One Box Set, at the main menu on the last disc, move down to the last option and then move right. The HBO logo will appear out of the blackness. Click on it to see a list of HBO credits."

The amount of linear content used in *computer games* varies from game to game.

Stories often set up and conclude the experience. In Star Trek®: Bridge Commander™, as an example, all players see the same opening movie, but depending on how they do, might see just one of three concluding movies.

During the actual interactive portion, computer games are increasingly using extensive linear content. In Deus Ex, when you walk by an office, you can hear two officers arguing over the nature of government. You can keep walking, or you can stop and listen.

Most *sets* in computer games are linear. The fields or buildings or roads or bridges never change, except for maybe a door opening or lights flashing. (The Sims, in contrast, is an example of a game with dynamic sets.)

Most games also have what is called *triggers*. Very similar to the Easter eggs in DVDs, these are predefined, predictable moments when something irrevocable happens. They can be set off when a player finishes a level, reaches a geographic milestone, or even destroys a facility. Triggers can take you to a different level of play, expose you to extended pieces of dialogue or new scenes, introduce a new character, give you some new ability or tool, or even insert something as simple as a new message into the field of play.

For most gamers, these moments are a form of reward. They often represent completion and progress, and should represent some type of entertainment value in and of themselves. In Max Payne, game play stops as a door explodes off of its hinges in slow motion in a shower of glowing sparks. *The Last Supper* it is not, but it is an enjoyable moment that breaks up the action.

Story and other forms of linear content in computer games can be a mixed blessing in terms of longevity (the number of hours a player will interact with a game). While a strong story increases the enjoyment the first time around, it can drag down the experience each subsequent time. Hearing the same quote again, or seeing the same set-up again, or seeing the same hallway or dungeon can become tedious. It reminds users that they are not in as much control as they might have been led to believe.

In the world of traditional e-learning, most content is linear, and it comes in the form of stories, case studies, triggers, dialogue, and video. Most models of assessment around linear content are based on the playback and new applications of old content; for examples, look no further than the tests that we spent all of our school years taking.

Movies were hoped to revolutionize education, but never did (I could argue that they did revolutionize what we know, but that is a different story). Despite their power, they still are linear, with all the shortcomings that implies. "You might react to a particularly moving scene in a film," says Karl Kapp, assistant director at the Institute for Interactive Technologies at Bloomsburg University, "but the film doesn't respond to your actions; it is completely independent of how you react to it."

Linear content is still primarily the province of the creator, and thus the least valuable of the three content types.

Cyclical Content

WHACK!

A ten-year-old girl is hitting a tennis ball against a backboard. She spends hours hitting the ball again and again. She got up early to do this. Sometimes she hits lobs, but mostly it is the same two strokes, forehand and backhand. And with every hit she is making micro-modifications to her movements.

WHACK!

To her parents, her workout seems unbearably dull. "How can she do that all day?" they ask. "It's just the same thing over and over." They watch for a few minutes, and then get back to what they were doing.

WHACK!

The neighbors have learned to close their windows on that side of the house when she practices. This keeps them good neighbors.

WHACK!

The girl is learning, but it is hard to quantify what. How can her learning be tested when the change from morning to afternoon seem so small? What kind of test could be applied to validate or quantify this muscle memory? All anyone knows is that she is at the top of her local tennis ladder.

WHACK!

Her coach wishes more of his players were that dedicated. He uses her as an example. He asks the entire tennis team all to practice more off the court. But this? How could any coach, or teacher, or instructor force this kind of learning, this kind of relentless repetitive practice? It has to come from within.

WHACK!

We have all seen this same behavior in people interacting with computer games. They spend hours, and no one outside of their world understands why. This cyclical content is in the very DNA of computer games, born of their Pac-Man® and Asteroids heritage. People would spend hours in arcades burning through piles of quarters. With cyclical content, every mistake seems to a player, in retrospect, avoidable. Slight twitches mean the difference between life and death.

Midtown Madness is full of such moments. How quickly can you take a sharp corner without flipping? Can you hit the ramp just right to jump over the river? Every failure is an invitation to try again.

WHACK!

This is where most educational simulations will fail. Cyclical content has to be mapped to, and represent faithfully, a specific "real" activity. Teaching the right cyclical content assures that the content can be transferred to "real life" immediately and seamlessly. Teaching the wrong cyclical content, mapping to irrelevant interactions, will render many simulations, at best, academic.

WHACK!

Open-Ended Content

Eating well is difficult. It involves balancing several key variables.

There are calories. We need enough good calories, and we do not want too many bad calories.

There is time. It takes time to prepare healthy food. Just the chopping alone can drive you crazy. And you have to go to the store almost every day!

There is money. Junk food is cheap in the short run. There is a sale going on right now at the local supermarket on something deep-fried.

There is planning. To skip breakfast or not? What happens when a meeting runs late? What happens when the lunch counter closes and the only option is a vending machine? Crackers, nuts, or candy?

There is our energy level, which we have to monitor. Cut out food too quickly, and you don't have the energy to exercise. And exercising is critical. But if you exercise too much, you sure get hungry.

Probably the trickiest currency is our will power. We start off with a huge amount, but that windfall only is good for about a month. Then we have to earn it and spend it on a day-by-day basis. Eating less lunch may result in eating a candy bar or chips in the afternoon if we have spent our will power. Some of us look in the mirror, get depressed, lose will power, and then eat junk food for a short-term pick-me-up, making everything worse in the long term. There are always tradeoffs and unintended consequences.

Most importantly, there is no one answer. It is individual to each person. Even a person with perfect balance has to change around the holidays, or when traveling (especially to conventions), or when unforeseen circumstances pop up. The skill of good eating requires not just knowledge of what to eat, but when to eat, why to eat, and even how to eat.

This is the nature of open-endedness. And computer games capitalize on it in spades.

An open-ended experience is no longer just about the creator, but also about the end-user. As with a play in a small theater, it is a partnership. This is where computer games finally get out of the James Bond destruction mentality (your job is to destroy something incredible) and into the Thomas Edison mode of actually building something incredible (yes, all right, I admit, sometimes to destroy something else). Users can express themselves.

Open-ended experiences are accepted to be so desirable that every game designer claims that that's what his or her content is. But there are a few quick tests for open-endedness in both games and simulations:

1. If two people are successful, how similar are their solutions?
2. Does a person want to play again to try a different approach?
3. Finally, are artifacts created? Can people share a model built, or a map designed, or a house, or even a fabulous configuration (say for a car) with friends?

Open-ended environments are very good for developing strategies, building up environments, and taking ownership. Skills learned this way are the most easily transferable from situation to situation, and enabling these will be a necessary component of most future content.

Rethinking Content: What Should Be Taught?

These three content types, linear, cyclical, and open-ended, are the primary colors in our palette (seen in Figure 3.1). Any educational material needs to liberally use all three.

Figure 3.1 Simulations' Primary Colors

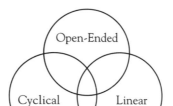

The instinct of any simulation designer is to repurpose the existing course material from academic and organizational classrooms into these three categories. However, most of the content that we have taught traditionally, especially history based, has no cyclical or open-ended counterpart.

Going from this black-and-white world of traditional instructional content to the vivid spectrum of content used in computer games (and, of course, life) will be the dominant intellectual challenge for all instructors in the future. And wouldn't you know it, our kids are already there.

Chapter Four

The e-Learning Arms Race

The most powerful company in the technology field doesn't software. It just advises everyone who does. Say hello to the Gartner Group.

—Selling Power Magazine, *May, 1997*

The year was 2000. I was the Gartner analyst who had launched and was now responsible for building their e-learning coverage. I would spend hours every day talking directly to training and business people all over the world.

Every call filled me with a certain dread. Could I help this person? Would I be able to really understand his or her problem, never mind offer some solution? I started listening to National Public Radio's *Car Talk* just to hear real pros field questions.

Sometimes I could give the client easy answers, or send them a report, which felt great. But more often we would brainstorm solutions together, which was harder and more nervewracking, but in the end felt even better.

I researched the market and wrote about it seven days a week. I produced detailed, specific, excruciatingly nit-picky vendor evaluations analyzing credibility and value (sometimes they were thirty or forty pages long) and broad, expansive, visionary papers for fun. I was also doing numerous press interviews with the largest magazines.

I was asked a lot of great questions, but also a few goofy ones. One of my favorites was, "What is the 'return on investment' (ROI) of e-learning?"

"Thirty seven point two percent," I would reply jokingly.

"Could you send that study to me?" they would quickly ask, desperately, always surprising me, as if grabbing onto my answer like a life preserver, and I would have to mumble an apology.

Everyone seemingly wanted to know this number. As if any two e-learning implementations were the same. As if a high number and a low number would cause two different courses of action.

What is the threshold for you? I would always want to ask them. What number would make you give up the program, and what number would make you risk your career for it? Would 10 percent be too low? If I said "three thousand" would that make you invest more than "negative five"? It was a question that typified a need for easy answers that we were expected to fill.

A favorite question from the press was, "What is the most leading-edge use of e-learning?" No matter what I answered, the next question was, "Can you give me four or five examples of companies that are doing it that I can talk to?" There were two problems with what they wanted. First, by definition, only one or two companies were doing it. And second, also by definition, they did not want to talk about it because they viewed it as strategic.

Still, these questions at least introduced some great conversations and challenged some widely held assumptions. They started everybody thinking.

Breaking Vendors

Another favorite activity in my analyst days was vendor briefings. e-Learning and training companies would come into my office for a few hours to present updates on their services. They would bring a small team, armed with thick slide packages, more often than not tailored for Wall Street analysts. Few of them realized that, from my Gartner vantage, I was more interested in what they would do to meet customer needs than in how they planned to achieve profitability.

The vendors and I would start off with opposite goals. They wanted to convince me how wonderful and unique they were. They wanted to paint an image of how they were poised for spectacular growth. They wanted to highlight examples of deliriously happy customers using their services.

And my goals? I only had one. I had to break through to the real story.

Most of the time, it was pretty easy. I might have recently talked to a livid customer. Or to some competitors who won a big account away from them. The vendors often gave me the ammunition themselves.

They might say something like, "We are the best-kept secret around." This meant that they couldn't even get in the door of many organizations.

Or they would show me their product, and something would go wrong. I would try to facilitate this "going wrong" process, of course. One way was to force them to deviate as far as possible from their script. "What if you press that button?" I would ask. "Now go here." The smoother presenters, if something went wrong, would try to say casually, "Oh that's right, I have the old version," or, "Hmm, this must be the new beta version." The others just turned red. But it didn't matter in the end. I knew I could drill in on product maturity and stability.

With the younger teams, the process usually lasted less than ten minutes. The more experienced teams, especially the seasoned CEOs, were much harder. It was like playing racquetball.

"I heard you lost the account at Company A," I would slam at them.

"It was political. The senior executive had a personal relationship with our competitor. And our competitor was willing to lose money on the deal, which we, being healthier, don't have to. But it is doomed. They will be back within the year," the vendor's CEO would slam back, leaning back in the chair.

"I was talking to a few organizations that were having trouble with your integration," I would serve at them, leaning forward.

"Ah, yes. That wasn't really *our* problem after all. Microsoft/Oracle/SAP had a serious bug in their server application software that they recently fixed in a free patch. That took away all of the issues," they would return.

And on it would go. Back and forth, sometimes for up to an hour.

Once the smoke cleared, my work began. My point was not to "get" the vendors or take cheap shots. I didn't even want to learn that much about them. What I needed from each company was knowledge about vendors that were tangential to them, including their partners and potential partners. I wanted a virtual classroom company to tell me about a learning management system vendor, and vice versa. They had the real information, and they were willing to share it.

All of these perspectives gave me a very clear take on the entire industry.

It was a great job, and I was well recognized for my efforts. Yet, the entire foundation was rotten. And that was e-learning content.

A False Assumption

Imagine a married couple. Every day, the husband tells the wife to change.

"Don't spend so much," he complains one week. The next week, he criticizes, "Don't talk so much at parties, and don't wear that dress." Then, twenty years into their marriage, the husband looks at his wife one day and says with disgust, "You know, you are no longer the woman I married."

As an industry, we were at the beginning of our marriage to e-learning. But already the nagging had been incessant—and leading the wrong way.

Many of the buying organizations I talked to were in the process of choosing a content vendor. And most of these basing their choice on four criteria:

- Volume of courses;
- Low cost per user;
- Ease of deployment; and
- Virtually any metric. (I'm serious. It could be the number of people who logged in, launched a course, or finished a course. It could be anything that resembled a statistic for all some of these people cared.)

Buyers didn't factor in quality at all. It was just too hard for them to figure out, or too subjective, or they (don't laugh) just assumed it to be there.

The shortsightedness of most e-learning buyers caused the equivalent of the arms race within the vendor market. They all began bulking up on content, building or purchasing titles as fast as they could. Vendors talked about hundreds or thousands of courses as being a good thing. Having fifty or sixty courses was considered competitively insufficient, even if the courses were better by any standard. Tina Sung, CEO of the American Society for Training and Development (ASTD), would later quote an estimate in her TechKnowledge 2003 conference keynote that there were 650,000 e-learning courses out there.

To compete, almost all e-learning vendors began outsourcing content development to low-cost, offshore suppliers. They outsourced not just the last levels of finishing, but also all aspects of the design process.

Content vendors, always savvy, began worrying about a long-term erosion of support for their content as both the tracking and anecdotal results were coming in and began pushing very aggressively for longer and longer contracts at lower and lower prices. I had seen some five-year content commitments for dirt-cheap prices.

Synchronous e-learning, in which a class would happen live while students, anywhere in the world, would listen, watch, type in questions, or even raise their virtual hands to be called on, all through an Internet connection, became more important than the virtual workbooks. This eroded many of the early benefits of e-learning, including scalability and automation.

So-called "blended models," where classrooms and e-learning were used together, were just becoming popular because self-paced e-learning content failed to be sufficiently useful. Essentially, for many organizations, e-learning became pre-reading.

I wrote research notes to help frame and motivate anyone who was considering being more ambitious. I talked about simulations, computer games, and the lessons that could be learned. I tried to provide air cover for anyone interested.

I also proposed a deal to the industry: "Help me find a great piece of e-learning content. Help me identify just one course that I could show anyone to get him or her excited about the potential of e-learning. I need a role model. For any vendor, I will be a free spokesperson. I will do everything from my bully pulpit as a Gartner analyst to get out the word. I will call magazine writers. I will call training directors at large companies. I will write favorable research notes. I will show demonstrations at conferences at which I keynote."

But both strategies—nurturing content-rich e-learning through research notes and finding a role model to extol—failed. I don't think I motivated anyone to begin a simulation project, nor could I find anything existing that met my own criteria.

This left me in an awkward position as an analyst. I could continue to be an enthusiastic spokesperson for an industry that I knew to be flawed. This, while morally questionable, had the advantage of positioning me to find lucrative consulting gigs with vendors.

Or I could become a professional curmudgeon and be forever whining.

Or I could leave Gartner, get my hands dirty, and directly contribute with a team to solve the problem. I would be doing the thing that any analyst most fears—becoming vulnerable.

I chose the latter. It seemed macho. It seemed exciting. It took me back into building something.

That something would be a simulation eventually called Virtual Leader. And like so many others, I am glad I could not see what was ahead of me or I might never have walked out of Gartner.

Chapter Five

The Myth of Subject-Matter Experts

From my perspective, simulations are best used
in four ways.

First, they are ideal for developing an
understanding of big ideas and concepts—those
things for which experience alone can deepen
understanding.

Secondly, I believe simulations are great for
dealing with time and scale. The computer gives us
an opportunity to speed up results of an action that
might actually take several lifetimes to play out.

I think simulations are good for situations where
it is important to give people practice in decision
making before it is faced in a dangerous or critical,
real-life situation.

Finally, simulations are wonderful resources for
taking us to a time or place that we are unable or
unlikely to experience directly.

—*Jane Boston, General Manager, Lucas Learning Ltd.*

Using some connections from both my current and previous jobs, I
became involved in a team that had most of the financial resources
and access to talent that we would need. Our entire reason for existing was wonderfully clear—to produce a single example of fabulous content that role modeled a new approach to building and
using e-learning.

Clear. Just not simple.

We picked the topic of leadership. Leadership is a critical skill that was widely needed by a large percentage of an organization. It was also an area for which, when I was a Gartner analyst, I was frequently asked.

"We tried this and that, Covey and Kotter, and nothing works," clients would tell me in. "The stuff is too confusing, too high level, too academic. There are too many charts that don't make any sense." Then they would lower their tone to a confessional level: "We know we have to take a more proactive approach to leadership, but we don't know how. Right now we hire leaders instead of nurturing them. If someone internally pops up as a leader, it is by chance. There are many people who would like to be leaders but don't know how. And we worry that we will lose them if we don't help them."

The external need was there. Also, bluntly, and please don't tell anyone, but it was a skill that seemed to be in short supply in most organizations with which I had personally been affiliated.

We developed a list of guiding principles for the project:

- We would borrow as much from the computer game industry as we could, while maintaining content integrity.
- We would represent an integration of the three different content types: systems, cyclical, and linear content. Each type would have to be used to exemplify and stretch their educational potential.
- The method and the content had to teach leadership in a way that would be as relevant to a line worker as to a CEO. This was critical. I personally needed to use it to convince decision makers: "Mr. or Ms. CEO, don't trust me. See for yourself." But I also wanted it to appeal to as broad of a group as possible. I did not just want to appeal to the B-school crowd or the high-potential employees. I wanted an approach for the masses.
- It had to be practical. If you learn something and don't use it in two weeks, it is gone. Early and frequent use of a skill is the

only way to internalize it. One of the most powerful lessons about public speaking is that you can practice it whenever you talk to anyone. We needed a similar approach to leadership. It had to be big enough to be relevant, but also in a form that could be used the afternoon after learning it.

- It had be gender neutral and easy to control by gaming standards.

The Tough Questions

And so the challenge was in front of us. If you were to design a leadership simulation, something that had both valid learning and computer-game-like interactivity, how would you do it?

Other than playing more than my fair share of computer games, I was way outside my domain of expertise now. I knew the existing e-learning market inside and out. I could draw market diagrams on a whiteboard in multicolor. But going this far out rendered much of my own hard-earned specifics useless. Not only did I not have any answers to the tough questions, but I didn't even know what the tough questions were. Some of the issues we did know that we had to solve were

- What would a leadership simulation look like when it was finished?
- Where should we start?
- How long would it take?
- How much would it cost?
- What would the perfect team to pull it off look like?

The Shrinking Role of Linear, Branded Experts

Our first goal, we agreed, was to find a leadership expert from whom we could license some established content. Our focus would be on the creation of the simulation, not on the leadership theory. We wanted to stick to our core competency. We figured this should take about a month to do, two months on the outset. Once we had done that, we could get to the business of making any necessary tweaks to the material, and then we would bring in the people to develop the software.

There were a few problems.

We visited with twenty or so academics, authors, and consultants. Some you would have heard of, most probably not.

They all had modern glass and chrome offices or comfortable, Georgetown homes. They all could not have been more gracious when we walked in the door. They were well-dressed, and I am sure they all played golf. They moved quickly and efficiently, belying their age. The conversations started off with pleasantries, although salted with numerous reminders of how busy they were, frequent checking of their watches, and reiterations of how much of a favor they were doing by meeting with us.

It would have been more encouraging if I could write that the experts fell into one of the following groups. In fact, everyone we talked to fell into ALL of these groups.

Group 1: The Figureheads

The experts wanted a huge amount of money for no work and no accountability. The first thing they made clear is that they expected five to ten thousand dollars a day in consulting fees, as well as huge amounts of equity in the company. A project like this would take weeks of their time, they calculated gleefully, maybe months. And they were very busy.

Group 2: The Control Freaks

These experts wanted complete control over the project. Or they wanted veto power at every point along the way, from product to marketing to packaging. They did not want their names misused, but they also wanted their names on everything, in the largest letters. It would really be their simulation, they decided, and we would help them make it. They would use their names in the title, and we would get a "powered by" mention on the back. And of course, they should have the right to infinitely hold up the project. It was their project, after all.

Group 3: The Pass-Off Masters

Could they help us? Well, maybe. They wanted to clarify what they meant by "their" time. They were very busy. What would be better, they explained, was to have their assistants/grad students help us. The experts assured us that these junior players, although only part of the team for nine months, were masters of the topic and would be our primary contacts for work going forward. The experts would still be there, however, to sign off on everything, when they could find the time.

Group 4: The Time Challenged

These experts let us know that they were on a different time schedule than we were. Returning a call after a month was hurrying for them. They all had critical projects, critical clients, critical family obligations, and critical month-long vacations where they would be out of touch. The academics thought in terms of semesters and five-year grants. Weeks were rounding errors.

Group 5: The Linear Headliners

Essentially, these experts viewed themselves as star athletes, and we were Wheaties®. They wanted their pictures on the box and a check with lots of zeros for the honor. Anything that didn't fit that mold didn't quite fit with them.

That mentality was difficult for all of us. But, we conceded, all of those were ultimately manageable.

But when we went a little further with a few of them, something that should have been obvious was staring us in the face. These people, self-proclaimed "experts in the leadership area," were all linear experts. Their knowledge consisted of case studies and high-level charts. They spoke in terms of sequences. They returned to linear content like a magnet to north.

To launch the simulation, they mulled, maybe a fifteen-minute video of them talking would be best. Or maybe longer. After someone made a mistake, they could come back in and give some comforting comments. They had some white papers that could be pre-reading, so players could read fifteen pages if they made the same mistake twice.

Meanwhile, the more probing questions we asked, the more they shrugged their shoulders. After hearing one person's dramatic case study, for example, we asked, "What determines a person's loyalty between friendship and authority?"

"No," she corrected. "As I said, friendship was more important. The authority never had a chance."

We persisted, "Under what conditions would those people have followed the authority, and not the personal relationship?"

"Well, that would be a different example. I would use an example from IBM in that case."

And on it went.

Today's experts are in the business of producing linear content—be it a speech, a book, or a lecture series. This linear framework has influenced how they gather information for decades. Everything they have ever studied was broken into paragraphs. Their mental note cards were ordered and re-ordered depending on the output. Getting any of them to think of content non-linearly would be a huge undertaking, possibly impossible. Because for them to accept The Simulation Way, they would have to accept that they were no longer experts. And that would mean no huge fees.

Sprinting in the Dark

As we wrestled with the experts, I thought back to the number of e-learning companies that tried to partner with or were spinoffs of big brand business schools, such as Fathom.com, Pensare, NYUOnline, UNext, Cognitive Arts, and Ninth House. Most were either out of business, on the ropes, or sold.

I am sure that all of these organizations had the expectation that the branded subject-matter experts would add value at several points:

- They would provide a lot of content;
- They would be involved in the development of the product to shape a better experience;
- Their faces would adorn the website to add credibility; and/or
- And they would even push the product to their clients.

In the cases that I later learned about in more detail, these assumptions turned out to be false. In fact, the opposite often occurred. For most vendors, the simple act of procuring a brand name took months. Further, their involvement easily cost (in both time and money) 15 percent or more of the entire project's budget. That was *money taken away from development.* That was *time* taken away from development.

Concurrent with my own experience, I was told by others that the content they provided tended to be war stories or notes from upcoming books and speeches.

They routinely added months to development time. Most changes tended to be egocentric. They wanted more videotapes of their talking heads being witty.

Imparta's CEO Richard Barkey accurately summed it up this way to me, warning of the dangers of experts who were only peripherally involved: "You can't create anything useful from a PowerPoint® pack and three days snatched from busy B-school politics."

And yet the siren of brand name academic stars continues to wail to this day. It almost consumed us. Few e-learning companies can resist the temptation of the illusion of credibility that the big names promise to provide, even though it often costs them their business.

Here's a recent example. Daniel Hamburger, then chairman and CEO of Indeliq, told me quite accurately, "A lot of players have been attracted to gurus. They are trying to borrow their credibility.

This is not a media business. It is as if they see whom they can get, and then build a course around them." Soon after, Indeliq ratcheted up their PR around an alliance with Babson College. And soon after that, Indeliq was absorbed back into Accenture, another company dashed against the rocks, and Daniel was no longer with Indeliq.

We knew we would have to try something different. We had to re-cast leadership. We also had to tear up our old schedule. So much for sleep.

Chapter Six

The Search for Content

I would not give a fig for the simplicity this
side of complexity, but I would give my life for
the simplicity on the other side of complexity.
—*Oliver Wendell Holmes*

If we were to build a leadership simulation, we needed to start from scratch. Our first step was to, locust-like, devour every scrap of leadership content we could find. We spent several months at the end of 2000 and the beginning of 2001 doing nothing but research.

We revisited people from our old lives and used them to help us identify academic, corporate, and political leaders. Everyone pointed us initially to the people with the most power. It was only through prodding that we got to the bottom-line people as well.

We rented out hotel conference rooms and called together focus groups. We gathered groups of people, sometimes organized by industry, sometimes by position. We asked these identified experts questions such as:

- What is a situation that needs leadership?
- What are some strategies or techniques that you use? What happens if you do not use the strategies? How do you know whether you are successful? What is the cost, even if you are successful?
- When do you decide not to exercise leadership?
- What are some common traps?
- How do you know whether a situation is going well?

We also did a lot of indirect research. We read hundreds of books, articles, and speeches. From that, we culled thousands of what we considered to be raw "leadership" observations, from sources ranging from Oliver Wendell Holmes to Robert Redford in *The Candidate*, from Tom Peters to the *Tao Te Ching*, from a CEO of a major pharmaceutical to the person who drove his car.

Here are some examples:

> Bring humor into the workplace where possible. Laughing eases tension and stress and reduces anxiety levels. It also makes for a more personalized work atmosphere.
>
> —*Bob Adams*, The Everything Leadership

> The best way to have a good idea is to have a lot of ideas.
>
> —*Dr. Linus Pauling*

> Czarnecki was just a very nice guy, too nice for the new IBM.
>
> —*Doug Garr*, IBM Redux: Lou Gerstner and the Business Turnaround of the Decade

> Bob . . . had a million ideas and brought new life to the position.
>
> —*Jack Welch*, Jack: Straight from the Gut

> You're always more creative when relaxed.
>
> —*Lighthousewriters.com*

> There is nothing like the sight of the gallows to clear the mind.
>
> —*Motorola's Gary Tooker*

Write up your idea in a memo. People may roll
their eyes if you bring a written handout, but at
least there won't be any doubt as to whose it is.
—Sarah Myers McGinty, Ph.D.,
quoted by Anne Fisher in Fortune, *2001.*

Sometimes those who refuse to cooperate actually
have valuable knowledge or abilities; they may
even be indispensable to your success.
—Eliza G.C. Collins and Mary Anne Devanna,
The New Portable MBA

Appendix One contains a small sampling of the massive collection of leadership quotes that we had to ultimately organize.

Leadership Activities

The more we discussed the issue with practitioners, the more we read, the more the office walls filled with sheets of quotes and diagrams, the more depressing it became. It seemed that so many of these activities were contradictory, or impossible:

- Leaders are essential to an organization, and the world.
- Leadership is inward resolve, and/or outward motivation.
- Leaders add humor to a workplace, and/or/then get everyone revved up.
- They speak with authority and conviction and/or/then listen well.

It was like reading the Bible trying to distill the ten commandments. A president during a war was a leader, and so was a parent helping his or her child to scribble creatively.

We made some progress, even if it did not feel that way. We identified a range of activities that a leader might have to do, which also were seemingly at odds with each other.

The list of leadership activities included:

Align work with an organization's values

Ask key questions and focus on the key facts

Assess character of different groups, the values and concerns they embody, and what competing agendas create barriers between people, departments, and divisions

Attack the unproductive

Bring a quiet person in

Bring about active engagement

Bring people together

Consider the appropriateness of a solution

Create an environment that enables work

Demand compliance

Develop person/people

Discover new ideas

End meeting and get on to the work at hand

Find common ground

Focus on the important work, not the distracting work

Find the big picture perspective

Give the work back to the people

Help the other people who feel frustrated

Identify correct ideas

Identify the challenge

Introduce information

Listen to the lone or discordant, silent, or not physically present voice

Lower tension

Make friends

Manage the group "mood" and ensure that the climate of trust is maintained

Mobilize toward a vision

Neutralize a cancerous person or idea

Raise a person's stature

Raise tension

Recognize and gain formal authority

Remind people why their work is important and necessary

Structure the conversation

Successfully introduce an important idea

Switch the current idea

Uncover consensus

Uncover the underlying issues

Wait out any chaos

Where necessary, go against the grain

Work on an idea

Dynamic People Variables

The volume of input was getting overwhelming. It was even worse on one of my early pet issues, which were the variables we would need to use to define characters in a simulated environment.

For example, what combination of variables would make a person yell at a meeting instead of cry, or praise someone instead of criticize him or her? What would push a character from one state to another? Or what would change in a person that would make him or her look out the window versus be engaged? We had to be specific.

Some of the variables on our list to consider included:

Teamwork skills

Salary

Position of authority

Speed

Tenure

Capacity to learn

Energy

Charisma

Networking ability

Net worth

Intelligence

Character

Tendency toward deference

Willingness to trust

Job satisfaction

Resilience to change

Network of friends and allies

Tolerance of risk, competency in soft and hard skills

Tendency toward brown-nosing

Tolerance for special projects

Empathy

Conviction

Hypocrisy

Competitiveness

Spectrum of emotions

Openness to people and ideas

Curiosity	Age and gender	Relationship with
Ambition	Minority/majority	others (whether
Selflessness	status	inside or outside
Feeling that they were heard	Argumentativeness	the group)
	Assertiveness	

Deeper Logical Strategies

As we gathered tidbits, we still weren't seeing the simplicity on the other side of complexity. We had originally hung all our data points on the walls of our office, but pretty soon we had too many layers and we needed too much tape just to hold them up. My degree was in artificial intelligence, and some of my experience at Gartner was around knowledge management. Both disciplines had turned out to be too complex too model. Was leadership, also, just too complex?

We started to do some higher level organizing. We began to attempt to write some leadership rules in terms of very high-level code. How might a computer view a leadership situation? What would they have to see, and how would they have to react?

We didn't know whether it was a waste of time, but we hoped it would help us organize and focus. Here are a few examples of the rules we came up with. In the end, we wrote more than one hundred of these. They ended up forming the deep logical structure for Virtual Leader's artificial intelligence.

When You Are Not an Authority, Partner with Someone Who Is

When . . . you are not being heard; an authority figure is running roughshod; you perceive glaring incompetence, or something that violates values; and you need to pass on information to someone who is in a position to use it more effectively than you can or build a rapport with someone in authority:

You should . . . partner with boss, or boss's boss; leverage any authority gained by having had access to pertinent information.

If you do . . . you upset authority that you circumvent. You might be perceived as brown-noser or snitch. This may jeopardize your job, and your loyalties may be questioned.

But if you don't . . . you are not heard, you are not viewed as a "team player," and a project/situation that you view as misguided or ill-conceived advances without your input.

When You Are an Authority, Confer Authority on Someone Else

When. . . you have to move on (your position changes, but you still have a stake in the work), and you have either personal reputation or lasting interest in the project, or when a potential ally is not getting any traction in the room:

You should . . . confer credit or decision-making power by praising the person publicly, praise his or her ideas, attack critics, or donate credit for ideas.

If you do . . . in donating credit, you don't get the informal authority boost, others may not accept new person who hurts your authority, people might try to neutralize your delegate, the delegate who gets authority can take it another direction and subvert your intent, and you may appoint a delegate who is incompetent.

If you don't . . . you may be overburdened if you don't know when to delegate.

But if you don't . . . if in an effort to protect your own formal authority, you don't see that there may be others who know more than you do, you could burn out and the work won't be done.

When You Are an Authority, Donate Credit for an Idea to Someone Else

When . . . you have formal, but little informal authority, your idea may have a better chance of success and group buy-in if you give credit to someone who seems to have a lot of informal authority, or when you want to elevate a person:

You should . . . build on something the person says or bring up a related idea, leading him or her to suggest a similar task.

If you do . . . you don't get the informal authority boost. You may forfeit recognition and miss a promotion opportunity. And the delegate who gets authority can take it another direction and subvert your intent.

But if you don't . . . people will not be engaged or take responsibility. Subordinates or peers will not feel ownership if you are not gracious in sharing credit.

When You Are the Discordant Voice Without Authority, Introduce an Idea Carefully

When . . . you have an important idea and no one else is in favor of it and you have no authority:

You should . . . introduce the idea cautiously and early, be prepared to drop it immediately, contribute to others' ideas, make friends, and reintroduce idea by picking up on another's points.

If you do . . . it will take time, and you may support people or ideas publicly that you don't support privately,

But if you don't . . . your idea could be automatically dismissed.

When Some Issues Are Unknown, Uncover Underlying Issues

When . . . there is tangible unease that cannot be directly linked to what's happening in the room; the group mood is somehow off-key; or if someone's silence, fidgeting, or sudden, enthusiastic or antagonistic participation or change in normal manner is uncharacteristic:

You should . . . make inquiries in a supportive tone and create a "safe" environment, lower the tension, increase the friendliness of the environment, have a one-on-one conversation during a break with someone who is clearly distressed/uneasy, don't let people "phase out"—bring in the disengaged, or bring up a related topic in hopes of surfacing the underlying issue.

If you do . . . you could distract from all current agenda issues, you could very quickly raise the discomfort level for an individual or an entire faction, or you could bring up a problem that may not be solvable or appropriate for discussion within the whole group.

But if you don't . . . what is festering may resurface later on, and undermine or derail a major issue. Partnerships and alliances could be compromised.

When You Need More Ideas, Listen to the Off-Tone Participant

When . . . ideas are being introduced by people with no authority or credibility in the rest of the group, create an environment that accommodates the off-tone voice; consider its value, but still dismiss it if it distracts from the work.

You should . . . make sure you involve or acknowledge all people at the table in working on the (your) idea, solicit and listen to the off-tone point of view, as one voice usually represents many others and there may be value in it.

If you do . . . the off-tone voice could be a waste of time, you might lose ground and have to start over. The off-tone person also can become the issue.

But if you don't . . . potentially great ideas can be lost, and this may represent a prevailing point of view outside the meeting group that will need to be considered.

When It Is Time to Create and Maintain an Environment Conducive to Work, Increase Tension

When . . . not much effort or attention is being expended, there is no discipline, there is an insistence on focusing on easy fixes, and people come in late:

You should . . . introduce provocative, contentious, controversial, challenging ideas, raise your voice, attack slackers, get personal, and make multiple quick attacks.

If you do . . . you can become the enemy.

But if you don't . . . work will not get done and complacency and a tendency to conduct business as usual will set in.

When It Is Time to Create and Maintain an Environment Conducive to Work, Decrease Tension

When . . . people are paralyzed or inert, anger or other high emotions are displayed by the group at large, or when people leave the room because they cannot stand the heavy atmosphere:

You should . . . allow or create space for a bit of levity.

If you do . . . the meeting could disintegrate or go wildly off-track in an effort to distract from the goal not being achieved.

But if you don't . . . tension freezes the group into inaction and despair, the environment is still charged with underlying unease, and you compromise your authority.

When It Is Time to Create an Environment That Will Allow for Constructive Disagreement and Debate as Well as New Ideas

When . . . huge contentious issues are present and the group is not comfortable or trusting, cooperative, or even listening, when the room feels "unsafe":

You should . . . work on easier issues (for instance, protocol or scheduling); build trust, establish your formal authority, then switch to the harder issues, and roll out an idea incrementally.

If you do . . . time is lost in the course of confusion and chaos and people accuse you of not dealing with the real issues.

But if you don't . . . problems won't be resolved.

When the Group Is Too Relaxed, Identify Boundaries

When . . . the comfort level is too high and people have settled into their roles and show no interest in other viewpoints; when you recognize that two competing groups have some common ground and that you can unite them; or when same groups continue predictable battles:

You should . . . step back and try to get the big picture, deliberately fracturing a faction whose interest overwhelms the rest of the group or squelches an idea.

If you do . . . groups could combine to outvote or overpower you. People could get too comfortable. Ideas could be automatically and predictably supported without sufficient exploration.

But if you don't . . . hidden issues might remain under the surface and common denominators and unifying factors (common values, interests) could go unnoticed.

When a Quick Fix Is Suggested, Determine Appropriateness

When . . . someone's issue keeps resurfacing and distracting from progress and is not at the expense of other ideas:

You should . . . make small, "quick" concessions in order to enlist the alliance of someone for the purpose of achieving an objective. If it is a simple matter that clearly bothers someone unduly, make small, "quick" concessions to make progress on the big issue. Listen carefully to the problem, and discern whether it requires further discussion or can be addressed separately or later.

Determine its relevance to the system.

If you do . . . you may put inappropriate attention to a matter of little relevance to the majority of the group.

But if you don't . . . the issue may be distracting and become a constant annoyance. You compromise your authority if you dismiss an issue too quickly.

When an Idea Is Distracting from the Vision, Refocus the Group

When . . . the team needs to be reoriented:

You should . . . remind group of purpose and reorient group toward long-term goal.

If you do . . . there could be confusion as to procedures, method, timing, priorities.

But if you don't . . . you might be missing a chance to enrich, enliven, amplify the vision by adhering to it so closely.

Sprinting in the Dark

Time was our enemy, as our budget ticked away. We were so far from where we wanted to be at this time. We knew we were making progress at understanding and framing leadership. But in another sense we felt further from the finished product than we had begun. We didn't yet have a single idea for a screen shot, or a model, or a way to pull everything together. We had wanted to begin conversations with early beta sites by now, but looking at our piles of notes, we wondered if we would ever get to that point.

Chapter Seven

What Would a
Leadership Situation Look Like?

Stages of the Cognitive Task Analysis process
comprise:

1. Identify the tasks that constitute the target
   performance for the job, that is, what are the
   important and difficult tasks associated with
   the job?
2. Determine the required skills involved in performing the target tasks, that is, what are the
   procedural skills and system knowledge required?
3. Generate the mental model used by the expert(s),
   that is, what are the strategies and problem-
   solving techniques employed by experts?
4. Identify the difficulties encountered by novice
   user(s), that is, what are common novice
   misconceptions and what knowledge, skills, and
   strategies do they lack?
5. Focus the teaching concentration, that is, which
   instruction components are most beneficial?

—*Ronnie Soles and Stephanie Lackey,* Planning
the Implementation of Synthetic and
Instructional Agents in Virtual
Technologies and Environments

Simulations place end-learners in selectively lifelike situations, requiring them to successfully manipulate some aspect of their environment. So far so good.

And if you are creating a simulation of a specific object, tool, or interface, such as a Volvo engine or a nuclear power station control panel, some design decisions are relatively easy. Basically, you would go through the stages of cognitive task analysis as, for example, Ronnie Soles and Stephanie Lackey describe for an AAAV gunnery station:

> The following tasks/procedures will be researched, and strategies will be developed to address each task with the VEAAAV-IA:
>
> Visually scan for targets
>
> Monitor detection systems
>
> Identify target as friend or foe
>
> Determine whether to engage target
>
> Prioritize targets if multiple targets identified
>
> Select target to engage
>
> Acquire target
>
> Select weapon
>
> Select main gun ammunition
>
> Lase target to determine range
>
> Determine ballistic solution
>
> Lay weapon
>
> Aim
>
> Fire weapon
>
> Observe effects
>
> Terminate engagement
>
> Monitor ammo in ready rounds

You would as accurately as necessary represent the controls and functionality. It would be straightforward to compare how well you did against the original.

But if you are tackling broader, more abstract skills, such as project management, ethics, algebra, electromagnetism, or nutrition, even knowing what to simulate suddenly becomes difficult. What will the end-learners be doing in the simulation? What will their goals be? What does the environment look like? How will the end-learners control the action? What is the action the person will control? How will anyone know whether what he or she is doing is right or wrong? In all of these cases, our classroom models are more misleading than helpful. Will Wright, creator of The Sims, wondered whether you could create a simulation to teach math without ever showing a number.

Getting the look and feel right is critical. The stakes are high. The boundaries are brutal.

If the controls are too *complex*, if the end-learner has to press ten different buttons to make anything happen, the learning curve will be too steep and few will engage it unless they absolutely have to. If the controls are too *simple*, such as pressing the one big red button at the right time, or a multiple-choice interface, the learning itself will be too superficial and feel too manipulative to be useful.

If the situation is too *concrete*, people outside of that one context will find it uninteresting. If you were doing a nutrition simulation within the context of an Eskimo family living off the land, potential users living in suburbia might find it hard to relate enough to care. Or if they did engage the simulation, they might find it challenging to take back important lessons to their daily lives. But the situation can also be too *vague*. Abstracting food into blue and red blobs to represent protein or fat, for example, could be equally hard to make relevant; no one, not even the Eskimos, would find that satisfying.

Meanwhile, if you present *too little* information to the end-learner, the person can become lost and frustrated. The user would turn on the simulation, have no idea what was going on, flail about, do badly (or worse, do well!), and end the experience with a negative feeling. If you present *too much* guiding information, the simulation becomes linear content with really expensive illustrations. The player then is just following instructions, never bringing in his or her own judgment or skills.

Finding the Right Game Genre

Our instinct was to look at existing computer games for Virtual Leader (although we weren't calling it that yet). Just as television shows come in genres, such as situation comedies, news magazines, reality shows, and dramas, so do computer games come in their own genres. Existing game genres have the tremendous advantage of being well-understood and accepted from both the designer's and the player's perspective. We would then be able to walk in with an understanding of the basic game play and just have to tweak some key relationships and graphics.

The approach of using an existing game genre as a model sat well with all of us. As long as we found almost any close-enough computer game genre, we figured we could bend the material to go the rest of the way.

We eliminated some genres immediately as having little or no potential. *Fighting games*, where players controlled a character intent on beating the stuffing out of other characters, didn't seem a natural path for what we wanted. Like so many genres, they reinforced the inaccurate but widely held view that computer games are intended to be primarily for adolescent males, which we knew we had to avoid at all costs. We crossed the fighting game genre off the list.

Driving and racing games such as Electronic Art's Need for Speed™ series were also ruled out. Neither the scenery nor the interaction with a vehicle added value to the leadership learning objectives we were trying to accomplish.

We looked at *puzzle games*, such as Wheel of Fortune® and Tetris®. These were fabulous from a gender-neutral perspective. And many early educational games already used these models, so we could build on past work. Besides, everyone with a computer has played solitaire. But while using a game veneer to dress up and quiz employees on content that belonged on note cards made the content a lot more fun, and probably made it more memorable, it was still transferring the same old linear content.

Platform games such as Earthworm Jim™ 3D and Tomb Raider™ likewise held little hope. These involved doing a single action over and over again, jumping or ducking at just the right time. *Adventure games* seemed too linear and also had fallen out of favor within the gaming world. *Role playing games*, while wonderfully open-ended, seemed too complicated and inaccessible to a casual, inexperienced user with all of their layers of screens and constantly modifiable abilities, and they promised minimal learning payoffs.

Sports games had an interface appeal. They were clever and designed for more casual gamers (Figure 7.1). There was a *rigor* to sports games; the designers had to replicate a very familiar situation, rather than a fictitious space battle or historical environment. The rules of the game had to match players' expectations. Sports games featured well-known athletes, so they used realistic people. This was all perfect, theoretically. But as we dug deeper, we realized that each specific game model, such as football or soccer, was so specific as to be untransferable. Using the game pad to run or pass did not translate to any leadership situation, no matter how we twisted it. They were a dead end path as well. Sadly, we crossed them off our list.

Figure 7.1 Electronic Arts Madden NFL™ 2003

First- and third-person shooters, evolutions of Doom®, seemed more appropriate. They could be exhilarating and almost lifelike. You play the game as a single character, looking through his or her eyes or over his or her shoulder, furthering the adrenaline buzz. They were incredibly popular and therefore familiar to millions of game players.

But for all of the running, and shooting, and explosions, and even in the so-called *first-person sneakers* such as Thief, the environments are pretty static. The interactions focus on either killing creatures of varying powers or finding keys and unlocking doors to new rooms or levels (full of more creatures of varying powers to kill). In the end, we did not find this to be a useful framework, and so reluctantly crossed the first-person shooter and sneaker genres off as well.

The Hope of Strategy Games

The last genre on our list was *strategy games,* including *real-time strategy (RTS) models* defined by Westwood's Dune II and expanded through Blizzard's WarCraft® and StarCraft® franchises. These held a higher potential. We included in this analysis *turn-based strategy (TBS) games* such as the Sid Meier's Civilization® series and my personal favorite, Sid Meier's Alpha Centauri™ (Figure 7.2). We also looked at many of the *tycoon games* here, such as RollerCoaster Tycoon® and Monopoly™ Tycoon™.

These strategy models provided a fabulous framework for Virtual Leader, we thought. Chess-like, these games put the player in the role of a disembodied, high-level general-type, with the task of balancing numerous, often-competing tasks such as resource gathering, production, research, consolidation, and expansion. (In fact, I had argued in a research note for Gartner that Alpha Centauri could be considered a business game, if nothing were changed but the graphics and a few other minor pieces of linear content.)

Instead of working to control geography as in Alpha Centauri, units in our Virtual Leader simulation could be battling for customers and accounts, so-called market or mind-share space. Once seized, this would provide long-term resources. Instead of buying bigger tanks, Virtual Leader players might hire and train better

Figure 7.2 Screen Shot from Sid Meier's Alpha Centauri™

salespeople or mount elaborate advertising campaigns. As for military success, technology and innovation would be expensive investments in the short term but critical in the long term for business success. Aligning technologies with strategies would be critical. As in Alpha Centauri, the complexity of situations could often result in interesting feedback loops or mini ecosystems. The law of unintended consequences could be everywhere.

But like everything else we looked at, the deeper we looked, the more even this genre seemed brittle. As with all of the other genre, strategy games had not evolved around encouraging game behavior that has a real-life counterpart. To be sure, they did a great job at teaching high-level systems thinking. And linear content would be easy to sprinkle throughout. But the interfaces were abstract; if we used them, we would lose the cyclical component, the "muscle memory," that we thought was so critical to making the skills transferable to the real world immediately and seamlessly.

Also, strategy programs would be too complex for a casual user. Too much action happens off-screen.

Finally, strategy games didn't provide a first-person experience. Players wouldn't be seeing the world through their own eyes. Even though we had rejected the first-person shooter approach, the first-person perspective still seemed emotionally critical to simulating and learning leadership practices.

Most importantly, when looking at everything, we worried that any of the familiar genres would overwhelm our content, forcing us down a path of greater and greater compromises. By simply putting on a new veneer of linear content and making computational changes to an old framework, we might make the game more acceptable to a business audience, but we really wouldn't be teaching anything substantially different.

We came to a conclusion that I believe all simulation designers will have to come to in the near term. Because the content has to reside at all three levels—cyclical, linear, and systems—we will all have to build completely new genres to populate the world of educational simulations. This is what Will Wright did when he created both SimCity™ and The Sims.

This realization was mature. I believe we skipped creating a failed generation. But looking at a blank computer screen, it wasn't very comforting.

The Meeting Was the Key

The first real breakthrough in our own design, a significant focusing of the material and a sense of minor accomplishment for our design team, came without our really even realizing it. As we talked about leadership, we continued to return to *meetings* as "moments of truth." They always seemed to be a leadership crucible, the place that best epitomized where leadership had to happen.

I think you will agree. A meeting is both focused and open-ended. It is also familiar in that everyone has been in a meeting. Some of us have actually been in more than one.

The meeting incorporates many elements of all leadership situations. There are allies and enemies. There is an agenda. There are hidden ideas, including issues like the proverbial dead elephant in the middle of the room that no one wants to acknowledge.

These realizations allowed us finally and blissfully to begin to define the Virtual Leader experience. We began to see a flow to the simulation.

There would be some opening sequence to define the situation. This sequence would be linear, possibly a segment where the player is reading emails or even seeing a video. The player might receive an order or instruction from his or her boss or hear about some crisis.

Then the player would enter a room full of people, with a goal or two. The player's mission could be anything from ferreting out a key issue, to pushing an idea through to acceptance, to simply identifying the key people in the room. We could even use the equivalent of head-fakes, when the player could be given a specific task from a colleague that turned out to be impossible or misguided.

The player would interact with the non-playing characters (NPCs or bots) by listening to the conversations, watching the body movements, supporting or not supporting the people in the meeting, and supporting or not supporting the key ideas being discussed. A meeting, we figured, would take between six and thirty minutes.

Ideas would play as important a role in a meeting as the people. Some ideas would be inherently right, and others inherently wrong. Ideas would have varying amounts of support. The maximum number of ideas for any given meeting would probably be ten or eleven.

Our thinking about possible scenarios led us into ever more complex and lifelike considerations. For example, we imagined a situation in which only one character could bring up a given idea. What if this person was very shy? If the player didn't get several things right, including asking the shy participant for an idea or creating a situation where the person felt free enough to suggest an idea, this idea would never even come up, let alone be debated.

In our office, over cold pizza, brainstorming situations was so fascinating because, unlike space docks or even a World Series, we had all been in these situations. We had all been the shy person with a great idea.

Also, for every idea, we would define how much work would have to go into completing it. There would be some ideas that were really big and would take a hundred units of work to complete, and other ideas that were very fast and simple, requiring only twenty units of work to complete.

So What's Actually on the Screen?

I was obsessed with the interface. How would this meeting be portrayed to the end-learner? What information would he or she receive? How would we visually represent and organize everything we were coming up with? How would the end-learner interact with the ongoing scenario?

Finally, we were able to put together some early sketches (Figure 7.3).

Figure 7.3 Early Interface Drawing

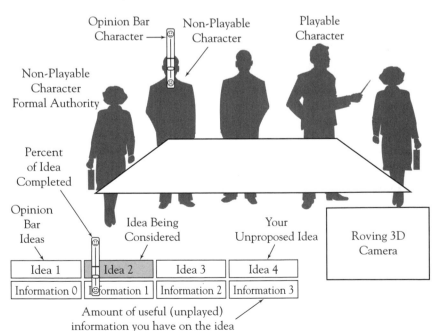

The player would be one member of a group around a table. We would use bars at the bottom of the screen to represent ideas.

Ideas would have progress bars that would move across the screen to show work being done. This would take advantage of the progress bar with which most computer users were already familiar. The user would be able to pull up idea bars and people bars, from which to express an opinion.

I also imagined, in the bottom right-hand corner of the screen, a special screen that would continuously be showing closeups of people's faces. That way we could conceivably highlight certain people, say if a person was zoning out or becoming really angry.

All this went up on our wall. It started to give us the cyclical piece, the minute-by-minute actions, our simulation would present. It excited us with a framework, but also terrified us because we realized how much was still missing.

Interaction

We kept on jotting down design requirements. The characters would have the ability to impact each other and the ideas. When interacting with either other people or ideas, we would have three different primary options: to encourage, to inquire, and to discourage.

The characters would have both verbal and nonverbal expressiveness capabilities. For example, if a character were mildly displeased, he might check his watch or yawn. If she was happy she might smile or nod. Characters could also berate one another or compliment each other.

Settings

We looked again at settings and at how the location of the meeting might influence what happened in it. Obviously a pick-up meeting in the hallway is different from a formal board meeting in an opulent setting.

We saw how any given setting could give power to certain characters, the home-turf advantage so to speak. If the situation were a meeting of diplomats, for example, it mattered greatly whether the meeting took place at an embassy (and if so, whose) versus at a café or even a taxi stand. We wondered how we might give the player the ability to change venues if things weren't going well, such as stepping out into the hall or even going into the bathroom to finish a conversation in a different environment.

Endings

Player/learners had to be able to experience different endings depending on how they did. Probably, we reasoned, we would have a good, a medium, and a bad meeting result. Or maybe even two or three bad endings, depending on what it was that made them bad. We would have to show the results of the meeting using linear content. As with everything, this ending content would be instructive as it reinforced what to look for in one's real life that signified leadership success or failure.

To research this, we went back to our various focus groups to ask about the results of leadership. They told us that the results of successful leadership were such things as:

Growth	Market share going up
More offices	Strong profits
More operations	Low turnover of customers and employees
Loyalty	
Good brand recognition	Higher stock price
Ability to adapt	Good public relations
Higher revenue per employee	High ethics
Sick days going down	High personal responsibility

They also gave us the consequences of unsuccessful leadership—this was before Enron and WorldCom, which would have given us more examples than we would have known what to do with. Some of the possible consequences they identified were

Someone moving the furniture out of your office

Empty parking lots

The IRS showing up

Massive layoffs

Bankruptcy

Family problems

Revolving door CEOs

Employee unrest

Depression or illness

Some disgruntled employee goes postal

Stock price takes a nose dive

Labor union problems

Whistle blowers going public

A *60 Minutes* team showing up

Honing a Theory:
How Do You Make Leadership Playable?

The cyclical and the linear pieces were starting to jell. But we were still missing the systems piece. The systems view would organize everything, reconcile contradictions in tactics, provide a framework for our artificial intelligence, help us determine what happens dynamically in a meeting, and frame our instruction.

Or, um, so we hoped.

Chapter Eight

Uncovering the Essence of Leadership

People compete, take sides, form teams, and when
one action is finished, members form new sides for
the next issue.

—*Hedrick Smith,* The Power Game:
How Washington Works

In the original SimCity, the user played a mayor whose primary
focus was to balance the needs of three constituencies: residential,
commercial, and industrial. These three groups sometimes com-
peted with each other for the player's graces, such as zoned land and
tax easements, in the short term, yet all three were necessary for
each other in the long term. The game had a persistent chart that
updated the player on how happy each of these groups was—like a
compass. Invariably, a player seemed to do well with only two of the
constituents at a time, at best.

As we grappled with the question of how to put the pieces of
Virtual Leader together, the three competing forces model exem-
plified in SimCity seemed very elegant. It had the potential to
shape the calculations, interface, and graphics. It was easy to ex-
plain to anyone who was interested, and it was not linear.

In real life, one of the best examples of a three-forces model is a
simple combustion engine like those in lawnmowers or weed trim-
mers. A combustion engine requires fuel, air, and a spark in order to
work. All three are necessary. You cannot overcompensate with one
to make up for a lack of another.

Looking over reams of paper and mountains of wall charts, we started asking the big question: Are there three equivalent forces at work in leadership? What are the forces that leaders need to control? We found three.

Force 1: Power

The first force was the easiest to identify. That was *power*. Power played a major role in every leadership situation. (Curiously, however, we later talked to one training group of a major consulting company that had not included power in their leadership model.)

Some people have power. And some do not. At times the wrong people have too much power. Some people spend all of their time trying to get more power. People use and/or misuse power. Power not used goes away almost as quickly as power spent toward the wrong goal.

As we delved into the nuances of power, we began to classify different forms. For example, power could come in the form of *formal authority*. That term covers a wide range of issues, ranging from salary and hierarchical position to the credibility that comes from writing a book or keynoting at a major conference. Some people called this form of power *organizational authority*.

Formal authority is relatively constant on a day-to-day basis. People do not often experience significant fluxes of formal authority in any given situation. Having said that, people who use all types of power well tended to gain more formal authority over time.

A second form of power comes from people having *allies*. We also called this informal authority, or "the group's opinion."

Allies might be long-time friends or people who happen to agree on a particular issue. Also, there are sometimes factions of people who always agree on everything, which provides a mixed blessing to any leader either inside or outside the faction.

Granted, there are many other subcategories of power. But for our purposes at this point, these two types—formal authority and the alliances formed within a group—seemed to cover power *pretty* well.

The result of power was straightforward as well. If someone with either type of power were supporting an idea, other people under their sphere of power would more likely support it based on nothing but that power. In the case of formal authority, if a boss was pushing one direction, the subordinates tended to go in that direction as well. If people had formed an alliance for or against an idea, it would be unlikely for one of them to go off in a different direction. Our thinking was, as U.S. National Security Adviser Condoleeza Rice would later say to capture it perfectly, "Power is nothing unless you can turn it into influence."

But then we began to realize that there was yet another kind of power that figured large in the kinds of leadership situations we were seeking to simulate. It was something that we had a hard time explaining. Here are some of its components:

- There is a power that is *earned* with coming up with a good idea. That is why some people are so insistent on identifying themselves with an idea.

- There is a power that is *earned* with being able to get work done, or at least being on the winning side of an argument. There is an oft-reported phenomenon of people voting for a candidate they know has already won so that they can be on the winning side.

- There is a power that is *spent* every time someone redirects (or at least tries to redirect) a conversation, either to a new topic or back to an old one.

- When someone tried to redirect the conversation without having that power, people started to get mad at him or her (the person tended to lose the group's favorable opinion). If he or she persists with an idea that no one else cares about or supports, even allies start distancing themselves from him or her, at least temporarily.

Grouped together, these became the final part of Virtual Leader's construct of power (Figure 8.1). We dubbed this third type of power *personal influence*. Others might call it political capital.

Figure 8.1 Types of Leadership Power

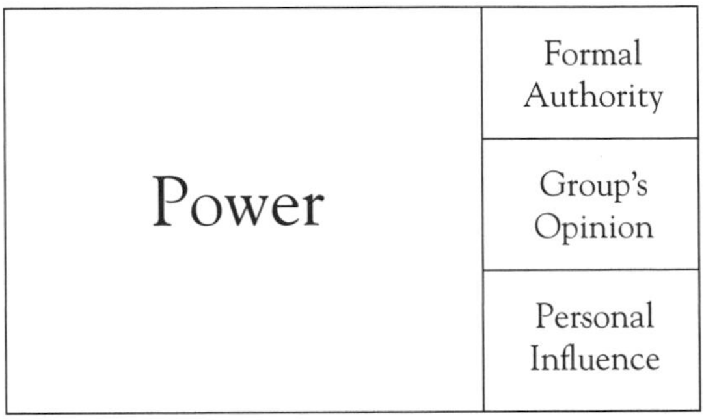

Power	Formal Authority
	Group's Opinion
	Personal Influence

Personal influence (PI) would end up being the most interesting type of power from a game play perspective, serving as an underground currency that gave intelligent wielders of it the ability to control the agenda. Some people work hard for the first two types of power, but the real pros, we saw, the people behind the curtains in real life, have mastered *personal influence*.

Leaders need power, of course. They need to build factions and coalitions. And leaders sometimes need to do horse trading to get it. Yet leaders don't need unlimited power, just enough. Anyone who spends too much time building a power base becomes manipulative and appropriately mistrusted, losing rather than gaining leadership potential.

Force 2: Ideas

The second leadership force we identified we dubbed *ideas*. Successful leaders need to get new ideas on the table. These ideas might be brought in from the outside or, as often as not, they could have been festering within the group for months (Figure 8.2). A group laughing, especially nervous, spontaneous laughing, is often a sign that some issue is just below the surface.

Figure 8.2 Ways Leaders Find Ideas

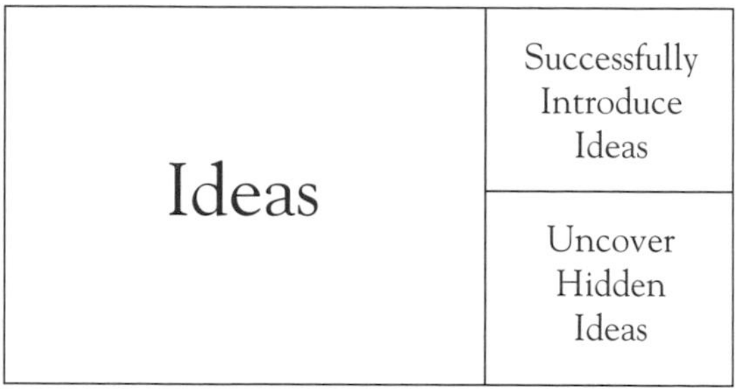

Ideas	Successfully Introduce Ideas
	Uncover Hidden Ideas

Ideas can be complex or simple, long or short, important or distracting. In the parlance of government, ideas are the bills. They are necessary to make laws, but they need a lot of support and nurturing. And they are elusive. Some of the best ideas might never be brought up at all. Just knowing how to bring forth an idea is an art in itself. Some ideas have to be introduced strongly. The leader needs to put all of his or her power behind them, making the case before any opposition can form.

Some ideas should be put up as trial balloons, floated to see whether they survive on their own. If you are the boss, you don't want to introduce an exploratory idea as a definitive idea. Your subordinates may make it happen, overestimating your own conviction. Or they may team up and shoot it down, undermining your authority.

If you are low in power (both politically insignificant and personally unpopular) you wouldn't want to introduce an idea you cared about in a way that too closely tied it to you. Sometimes, people introduce an idea as a negative to get it into the public forum without any personal association ("Some people think we should break for lunch, but I think it is too early."). In both cases, the person sacrifices any power that goes with the idea for the sake of the idea.

Leaders often have to explore contradictory ideas. This can be difficult if they have too early committed to one path.

More often than introducing the ideas themselves, leaders have to pull out the ideas that are in the minds of the other participants and put them onto the table for the whole group to consider.

And if some ancillary ideas are distracting some of the participants' full attention, leaders have to get those out on the table as well. Some successful meeting facilitators ask attendees to "check in" at the beginning of every meeting by saying anything that has been weighing on them. Just getting these thoughts out on the table, without having to resolve them, can put participants at ease.

This idea generating can be done through activities as dramatic as brainstorming or as simple as listening and asking probing questions. It requires sensitivity to the environment and the individuals.

Some people are most creative when relaxed. Others are most creative when very tense. Knowing which person is which matters.

Part of a leader's judgment has to be when to be satisfied with the number of ideas on the table. As with power, too much focus on ideas can prevent a group from ever actually getting anything done.

Force 3: Tension

The third force we identified for any leadership situation is that every member of a group has his or her own *tension* level.

People can be relaxed. They may feel they can't be fired no matter what happens. People can be tense. They might have learned that their jobs have been cut when they were wrong.

Leaders have two different goals for tension. This makes the force or tension a bit more complicated.

As alluded to in our idea-generating discussion, pushing a group toward the extremes of tension, either very relaxed or very nervous, can help the group to come up with new ideas (Figure 8.3). This is creative tension. As Rusty Rueff, senior vice president of human resources, Electronic Arts, puts it: "Most creativity comes at one of two times: When your back is against the wall or in a time of calm."

Figure 8.3 Types of Tension Leaders Must Manage

Tension	Relax
	Moderate
	Excite

But tension is also tied to productivity. People accomplish more when they are closer to the tension middle. Don't expect productivity when people are at an extreme. "When times are good you should talk about what needs improvement, and when things are bad you should assure people they will get better," said Anne Mulcahy, chair and CEO, Xerox Corporation, at the Executive's Club of Chicago, March 14, 2002. So once a leader has enough ideas, he or she must moderate tension to a productive level.

The interplay between tension and ideas is also interesting. Some ideas make people more tense just to discuss them. Other ideas make people more relaxed.

The ways in which a leader should moderate tension depends on both:

- What the current tension is, and
- Whether you want to surface new ideas or you want the group working productively.

Changing the level of tension impacts other issues as well. Yelling at someone might make the group like you less, but it can also make a group of slackers more willing to work.

Something Missing

Our three forces were a perfect beginning. They screamed "game play," as each could profoundly influence the others. Bringing up an idea could cost power and raise tension, for example. Yelling at someone could raise tension, making some people angry and others more creative. Yet they were only a set-up. There was something missing—a fourth force.

Geoffery Colvin, in *Fortune magazine*, December 10, 2001, summed up succinctly what we were looking for: "The main reasons CEOs fail is not mistakes in strategy or finance but simple inability to execute—to get done what they wanted to get done."

We had to add the concept of *work* to our leadership model (Figure 8.4). Work was what was done at the end of a day. Work was how a leader turned a bill into a law. People turn ideas into completed work. There was critical work. There was unimportant work that still needed to be done. There was work that gave a false sense of accomplishment. And there was work that outright prevented better or worse work from being done.

Figure 8.4 Work That Needs to Be Done

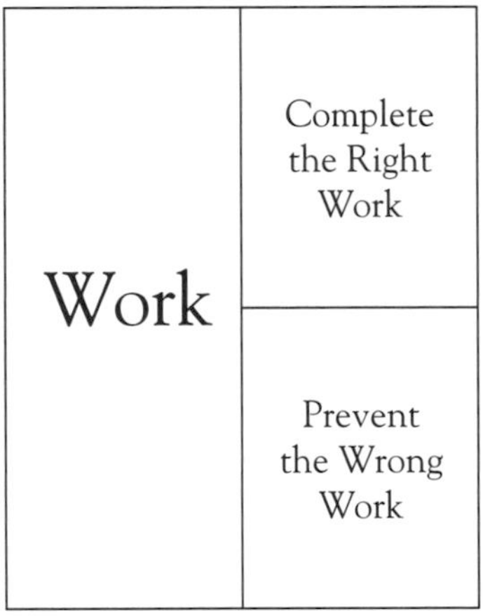

The Aha!

Could it be that simple? That straightforward? Could our three-to-one model be sufficient? It seemed that way.

Virtual Leader would be about the interplay of power, ideas, tension, and work—not necessarily in that order.

Gaining power, generating ideas, and moderating tension can be done in any order—or even at the same time. Meanwhile, the leader has to work with the group to evaluate the ideas being generated. Then the leader uses what has been built to get the work done (Figure 8.5).

Figure 8.5   Three-to-One Leadership

Power	
Ideas	**Work**
Tension	

In some cases leaders will spend all of their power, at least temporarily, to keep people focused. They will have to discard some great ideas. Tension may spike. But when the right work has been completed, all involved get a windfall.

Leadership as a Meta-Skill

"So leadership tells me when to use my other skills," one member of a focus group said. I was shocked. She was right.

We had defined leadership, without really knowing it, as a *meta-skill*—a skill about skills. We realized that the groupings of power, ideas, tension, and work could segment most training catalogues:

- *Power skills* included such things as negotiating, traditional sales, consulting, writing, and communication.
- *Idea skills* covered things like brainstorming, research, listening, benchmarking, root cause analysis, marketing, empowering, and strategic planning.

- *Tension skills* encompassed topics such as public speaking, dealing with difficult customers, stress management, conflict management, safety, change management, and sexual harassment prevention.
- *Work skills* included project and time management and streamlining business processes.

The task of Virtual Leader was to teach people when and how to use skills that, in most cases, they already had (Figure 8.6).

Figure 8.6 Leadership as a Meta-Skill

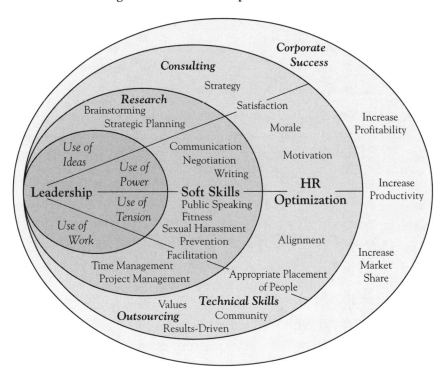

Another "aha" moment came when a director of training for a large bank observed that people, when enrolling in optional training, often focus in the one skill type area in which they are comfortable. People who are good at one power skill tend to focus on learning more power skills. People who like generating ideas tend to focus on other idea-generation skills.

At some point, if they don't cover the other three areas, more training actually makes them less effective, not more effective, employees. They become unbalanced, and therefore only effective if they are with a group, either deliberately or accidentally, that rounds them out from a "three-to-one" perspective.

The Question of Recursiveness

I knew we needed Virtual Leader to be useful at all levels of an organization. So we evolved our understanding with the three-to-one power-ideas-tension-work framework by explaining it to colleagues at all levels of different organizations. The response was very favorable. In fact, I found it easiest to describe our framework as a diagnostic tool for different levels of an organization.

About an employee, I would ask:

- Is he respected within the work group? If not, I would suggest that he work on better speaking or writing, perhaps even learn to negotiate.
- Is the tension too low or too high within her work group? If it is too low, visit a competitor. If it is too high, talk to some satisfied customers.
- Are there enough new ideas being considered? If not, brainstorm, research, and do long-term strategic planning.
- Is the key work being done? If not, consider brushing up on project management or time management.

When talking about a senior management team, I would ask the same questions in a different form:

- Are they respected within the company?
- Is the company as a whole too complacent or too nervous?

- Is the company actively cultivating and considering radical new ideas?
- Is the company accomplishing the critical work in the right volume?

Amazingly, the answers provided a specific blueprint as to what a senior team needs to do in order to better lead the organization. I can't say I was entirely comfortable when people actually initiated new programs based on our conversations, but I was encouraged.

Variations of the same questions could even apply to a CEO looking at an entire industry:

- Is his or her company respected within the industry?
- Is the industry complacent? Is the industry over-nervous?
- Is the industry looking at different business models? Different revenue streams? Bringing in new players?
- Is the industry producing the sufficient quantity of output to be sustainable and relevant? (This question might especially apply to young industries, monopolies, and government organizations.)

By the intelligence of the conversations that always followed these discussions, I knew we were onto something.

A New Take on Leadership

So at the end of the day, we had defined leadership as *getting a group of people to complete the right work*. Or had we redefined it?

It was not a definition that came to most people. But I liked the focus on the work, not on the individual. I liked how diagnosable it was. If someone was failing, an outsider could help determine why. If someone was succeeding, it was easier to distil best practices.

This new take on leadership was exciting. It opened up all sorts of possibilities. But it was also daunting. People had been studying leadership for centuries. Who were we to challenge everyone's prevailing views? Who were we to redefine a concept this fundamental? And if our simple view of this was so true-to-life, why hadn't someone else come up with it?

The short answer is that most people had come up with it. If you looked over almost any of the twelve thousand books on leadership, they contained our three-to-one elements. But because the experts were thinking linearly, the simplicity and depth of this model was never too apparent, nor explored very deeply. Armed with our linear content, our cyclical content, and now our systems content, we had the framework we needed.

Chapter Nine

The Lure of Linear Content

No one can tell you how to handle a particularly
difficult customer; you can't read a manual about
how to manage subordinates fairly but firmly. You
need to jump in and learn what works first-hand.
That's how leaders learn to lead. Reading all those
books on leadership won't do it. Only when you
find that your management approach results in low
morale and high turnover are you motivated to be
a different, more effective type of leader.

—*Roger Shank*, Virtual Learning

Learning does not happen when someone tells you something new.
We hardly can do anything new after just listening. The only jobs
where listening is sufficient for learning are those that require nothing but speaking and writing. For those of us who are not industry
analysts or college professors, it is more complicated.

There is a full cycle of learning, as relentless as the orbit of the Earth
around the sun, or Christmas advertisements in October (Figure 9.1):

Figure 9.1 Full-Cycle Learning

- *Start with an initial understanding.* People have an *understanding* of a *system*, which is to varying degrees incomplete. The broadest understanding might be summed up in the German word "weltanschauung," roughly translated to "view of the world." For example, one understanding might be a vague memory from an earlier trip that the hotel is about ten miles from the airport, just off the main highway, and the exit ramp is just after a movie theater.

- *Have a goal.* This is often initially communicated through linear content. It might be driving a car to the hotel from the airport, or a larger goal might have already parsed into smaller subgoals, like finding the current exit.

- *Formulate a plan.* Do this using your knowledge of your options and the environment.

- *Execute it.* This execution almost always takes place at the cyclical level.

- *Obtain feedback from the actions.* Feedback is not simply communicating good or bad, despite what some would like us to believe. In our hotel example, you might take the wrong turn when trying to find your hotel, but in the process you could stumble across a good restaurant, a good place to jog, or even the office where the next day's appointment is. That is the lesson learned, not just the sententious, "Next time, plan better." Mistakes are more educational than success in that they enable serendipitous learning.

- *Update your understanding.* Regardless of your degree of success in achieving the old goal, the loop is closed when you reflect on the feedback to update your understanding. Academics call this "reflective learning."

And the cycle continues.

The classic mistake of classrooms is to pile up huge amounts of un-internalized facts on poor students. Not able to confirm, modify, or reject each fact, the students either go into record mode, where taking notes becomes the end goal, or they shut down altogether.

Everyone reading this will have experienced far too much of both in their lives. Even the better week-long classroom experiences focus three or four days on queuing content, and then only on Thursday do students get to engage in role playing and experimenting to put their understanding to the test. By this time, it is far too little, far too late. (Role playing, by the way, is an incredibly high-pressure environment that forces traditional, not experimental behavior, which we will discuss later.)

Breaking the Challenge into Little Pieces

The workings of a simulation are similar to the basic model of the learning activity (Figure 9.2).

Figure 9.2 Workings of a Simulation

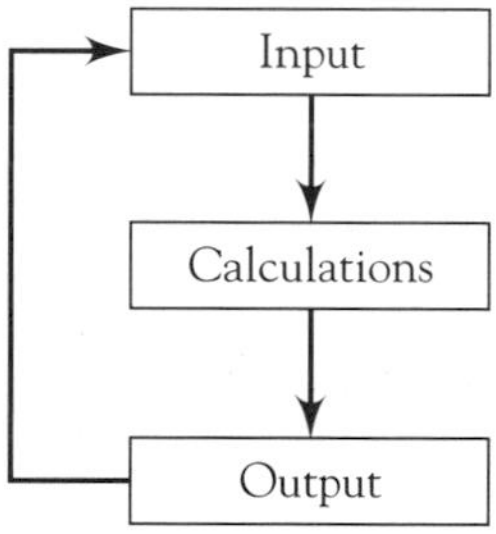

Users express themselves through their *input*; the simulation performs *calculations* and then presents feedback in the form of an *output*. Then the cycle repeats. In simulations, the speed of the input-calculations-output workings is ten, or a hundred, or even a thousand times faster than real life or the classroom's *understanding-planning-experimenting-updating* cycle.

Easy enough to understand. Much more difficult to do. There are also many different ways of achieving this feedback loop.

Why Not a Traditional e-Learning Simulation?

Work on our leadership simulation was not going well. Money was burning up faster than we had hoped. We had some ideas, some notes, and some schematics, but not, it seemed, enough for the massive production process that increasingly seemed to be required.

There was another way, however, to build a simulation. There was a strong contingent within the project team arguing for us to back away from our computer game model and make a "traditional e-learning simulation," the type used by Cognitive Arts (acquired by NIIT), Indeliq, and Ninth House. That way, we could get a few products out quickly. Once we had some success under our belt, we could plan the next phase to be more ambitious.

A Multiple-Choice Input Mechanism

Rather than a more complicated game-based input mechanism, my colleagues argued, we could use a simple multiple-choice type input. Users would be presented between two and five (or even more) options, and they would simply pick one from the list (Figure 9.3).

Figure 9.3 Multiple Choice Input from QuickCompliance

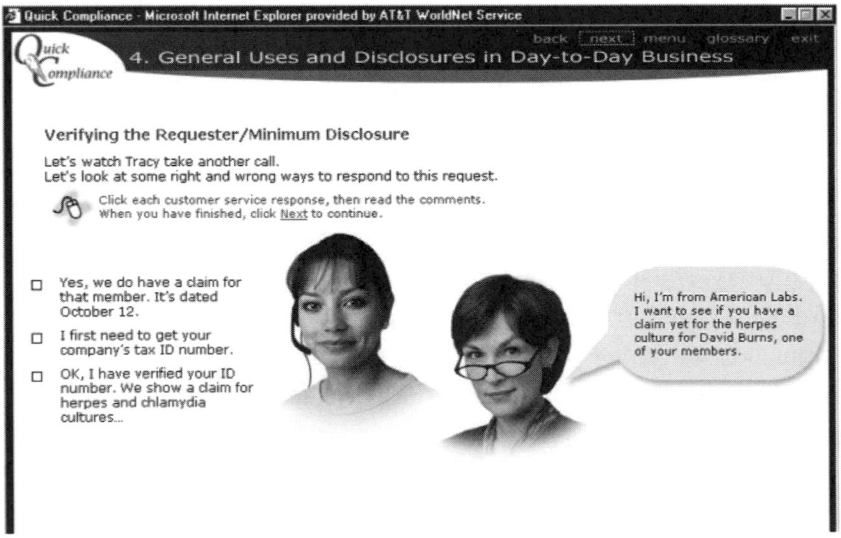

Multiple-choice questions could offer a lot of benefits to the end user, we reasoned. There would be no learning curve. Unlike computer games, everyone already knows how to use multiple-choice inputs. They are simple, making them perfect channels for entry-level employees and even CEOs who would not want to spend much more time than they had to. And they were cheap to construct.

We would have to be careful not to fall into some of the potential traps, such as these:

- We didn't want to lead the user too much.
- We also didn't want to railroad people into decisions that they were not committed to. "I don't want to say A or B," so many c-learners say. We would have to test rigorously to avoid that. We wouldn't be able to offer users total freedom to make strategic decisions, but we could create a good illusion.

One inherent aspect of multiple choice that we had to understand is that there is no time pressure to make a decision. Users can survey the situation, do research if they have to, and even try out some different possibilities before committing to an action.

The advantages are that multiple choices can promote contemplation, thoughtfulness, and reflection. They also lower tension.

The other side argued that the problem was that few choices are made in life that don't have some pressure associated with them. Another drawback of multiple choice is that some people are tempted to be more manipulative and try to psyche out the program.

A Branching Model of Calculations

Computer games use complicated calculations. That was the height of our ambition for Virtual Leader. But maybe we were making life too hard for ourselves. We didn't have to go that far. If we had a multiple-choice input, then perhaps the primary method of calculation could be some kind of *branching* schema (Figure 9.4).

Figure 9.4 Branching Schema to Simulate a Simulation

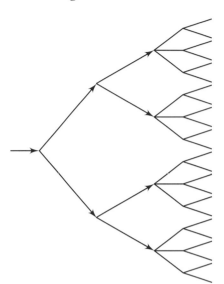

Telephone dialing is a good example of a *branching system*. Every digit is a branch, the order matters, and at the end you are at one distinct destination.

There had been a lot of research and examples already done using this mechanism. Few building them knew their true origin.

Branching storytelling was originally an interactive assessment model based on early military manuals. In these old manuals, engineers would be faced with a problem. They would be given a multiple-choice test, with each answer leading them to another page. On this new page, they would either be told they had the right answer and where to go next, or they would be told not only that they had the wrong answer, but also exactly why they may have been wrong.

While not technically a simulation, the branching models we were considering would at least be a simulation of a simulation. And would anyone really care that it wasn't the real thing? A branching model would provide a rich opportunity for stories, making some of our early content experts happy. Plus, a branching system, especially in contrast to a full computer game, is quite easy to create.

We talked over other considerable advantages. Because we would know exactly how someone arrived at a point, we could very precisely embed linear instructional content at the right time. The hand-holding factor could be higher than in a computer game model. We could turn up the tutoring if we had to.

We had to admit, though, that there were some problems. Branching experiences, true to their orgin, remain more assessment than experience. There are strict limits on what a user can and cannot do. And branching experiences can feel disjointed and manipulative if players feel trapped. Still, we saw those as challenges to our design, not as showstoppers.

Output of Video or Pictures

Clearly, an essential component of a simulation is the feedback it provides in the form of output. If we went down the branching path, we had two options:

Option 1: Light Browser-Based Output. Our simulation could have a browser-based output. We could teach leadership, delivered through the Internet to a standard browser, such as Internet Explorer or Netscape Navigator. We could use small sound and picture files. We could use Macromedia Flash-based animation. Plus, it would be easy to deploy and we knew a lot of people with skills in this area. And we could deliver it all over the world if we had to.

But ultimately the problem was that browser-based output could only provide a limited amount of feedback to the learner. It could still look only as good as or as interactive as a web page. We had to reject this format.

Option 2: Video. The other option for the output of our multiple choice/branching model was video. Video is probably the most familiar medium for Baby Boomers and has long performed the role of educator (with varying degrees of success), ever since the first documentary was created.

There were so many great advantages to video. The amount of detail and nuance are extraordinary. It feels serious and real. The over-forty people, having grown up with television, are very comfortable with it. It works well from a "dumb" terminal. And the body of knowledge around shooting and editing video is extraordinary. Plus, I personally knew the medium well.

There are also some problems with video. It is expensive. Huge bandwidth is required to stream it over the Web. Interaction with video has to be delayed (end learners can't actually interact when the video is running. They have to wait until it stops).

For me, another frustration was that video sows trodden ground. You can never be anywhere new with video. You are walking in someone else's footprints.

What's more, the density of information in video makes it hard to get it right. A few mistakes and the whole project looks like an infomercial.

Video can also be too specific for an off-the-shelf simulation, making it harder to extrapolate rules because the context is so strong.

Finally, it is hard to make small changes in video. If we wanted to customize anything, we would have to actually re-shoot a scene, if that was even possible.

The Decision

We debated all these issues, off and on, for more than three months. We conducted some video-based tests. We talked to users and managers who had implemented branching videos. We even made up some full-production video mock-ups. And we decided.

Branching videos have many wonderful qualities, but they have to be used in the right place. The multiple-choice interface and video is perfect for entry-level employee training, where very specific information needs to be conveyed, such as how to park a car for a rental car company, how to greet a guest at a hotel, or how to set a table at a restaurant. I have also suggested it recently to replace a safety seminar.

But for soft skills, skills that would have to be personalized and generalized across situations, it wouldn't work. It is too limited and was in conflict with too many of our early goals. We had to do it the hard way. We were going to hold true to our original vision of a game-like interaction.

Part Two

Modeling Reality

Chapter Ten

Rules for a Post-Textbook World

Simulation Design Principles

> What you want to do is create a game that's built
> on a set of consistently applied rules that players
> can then exploit however they want. Communicate
> those rules to players in subtle ways. Feed back
> the results of player choices so they can make
> intelligent decisions moving forward based on
> earlier experience. In other words, rather than
> crafting single-solution puzzles, create rules that
> describe how objects interact with one another
> (for example, water puts out fire . . .) and turn
> players loose—you want to simulate a world
> rather than emulate specific experiences.
>
> *—From a conversation with Warren Spector,*
> *creator of Thief and Game of the Year*
> *Winner Deus Ex*

With the branching video detour behind us, we went back to looking at the three organizing frameworks: input, calculations, and
output. It didn't take long to realize that we would have to make
more than just a single subsystem to handle all of the heavy lifting
that Virtual Leader had to do (Figure 10.1). We needed to build
separate systems to handle the key pieces—artificial intelligence,
the interface, the sets, the dialogue, and the animation, just to
name some.

Figure 10.1 The Key Pieces

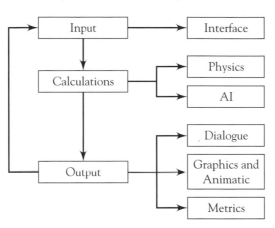

Defining Subsystem Characteristics

We couldn't design the individual subsystems at the same time, but we had to make sure they all would work together to achieve a common goal. It became critical to identify in advance the common characteristics of our subsystems to point them in the same direction.

All Subsystems Would Reflect and Enrich the Learning

Every component had to reflect three-to-one as the underlying leadership theory and meetings as the place where the rubber hit the road. This sounds easy and obvious.

Unfortunately, our desire for subsystems that enforced the core learning we had framed for Virtual Leader would minimize our ability to use generic components or frameworks developed for the computer game world. All of the techniques designed for typical pieces of a computer game—such as pathfinding (the AI required for bots not to get stuck in corners when they move freely) or collision detection (so things bounce off each other at the right time and in the right way)—did us no good, as they each reflected the needs of their respective genres. We were truly starting from scratch.

All Subsystems Would Reflect the Three Content Types

Each component had to be able to help us provide content that was:

- *Linear*, to deliver key bits of information;
- *Cyclical*, to map to actual leadership activities; and
- *Open-ended*, to reward the creativity of the user and encourage exploration.

We did not want any bottlenecks in our ability to deliver a rich learning experience. How closely these three content models came together at any given time would determine a large portion of the success of the simulation.

All Subsystems Would Have to Be Easy to Customize

It had to be easy to make small and large changes to all parts of the simulation. Virtual Leader would be an off-the-shelf, working application—a computer simulation ready to play and learn from. But ultimately leadership would just be one expression of our capability. The engine underneath had to be infinitely flexible, allowing customers to make both small and huge changes easily.

An organization should be able to change the relative strength of the characters' formal authority, for a small example, the military clearly uses formal authority differently than a dot-com start-up does. Changing that had to be as easy as turning a screw.

An organization should also be able to modify the program into a solutions selling tool, if desired. This type of complete rework would have to represent less than 10 percent of the original development effort.

The Question of Modularity

In the *Star Wars* themed game Jedi Outcast™, a player battles against thousands of the villainous storm troopers across twenty-five huge levels and forty hours of game play. But by switching out just one file with another, every storm trooper on every level will look different, talk differently, and even behave differently. That is the power of modularity.

For a working definition, *modularity* means that pieces of a simulation can be added, changed, or subtracted easily. A modular architecture makes massive amounts of customization possible, because the changes cascade automatically through the entire application.

With modularity, an organization can easily customize a large, extensive simulation. They can put in new characters, or maybe just change the voices of the characters they have. They could change the logo of a company in one place, and instantly have the change be reflected on every truck and every piece of stationery.

So far, so good. These would be difficult to implement, but relatively uncontroversial. We could both agree with and achieve these design principles in our subsystems.

Each would be easy to customize and both address the need for linear, cyclical, and open-ended content as well as be true to our three-to-one leadership framework and the idea that our series of company meetings would be the crucible for learning and practicing leadership skills.

There were other design issues, though, that were controversial. And unlike the first batch, these issues would become more controversial with time.

Do We Want an MMORPG?

One issue we grappled with was whether Virtual Leader should be a multi-player simulation. One of the biggest advances in computer games to date had been multi-player games, and now massively multi-player online role-playing games (MMORPGs), in which the game provides the environment and players provide the adversaries, were becoming more and more popular.

Many assume a multi-player educational simulation would be a better learning experience than a single player one. They assume that other people participating would make the simulation more realistic, more subtle, and of higher value.

Mostly, they assume wrong. Multi-player simulations have all of the problems of role playing. Here are just some of the issues:

- *Role-playing environments are highly public.* Most participants do not have the confidence or desire to try new behavior that might be more successful. Instead they resort to the risk-adverse patterns where they are most comfortable.

- *People in a role play don't act "normally."* People typically won't act petty, or territorial, or power hungry, when acting in front of a group. I have never seen a role play where people don't all agree at the end.

- *The logistics of getting people to meet at the same time is hugely expensive and time-consuming.* Someone has to coordinate. People have to pore over their calendars. Invariably people have to cancel at the last minute when a critical issue pops up. Training has to be flexible, because the real world is not.

- *Groups of people act differently from one another.* Some groups take it seriously, others joke around. This shrinks the number of people who have a common reference down to five or ten, rather than five or ten thousand, or even a hundred thousand.

- *There is no repeatability.* An end-learner can't try something ten or twenty or thirty times when other people are intimately involved. Human participants become exhausted and frustrated and bored. Computer characters (bots) never do. Ever. Actually, they are a bit annoying that way. Even if you play a thousand times, the bots are always ready for another round. They will never turn you down. People can wake up at midnight or two in the morning with a brilliant new strategy, come downstairs, turn on the computer, and the participants will be ready to go.

- *Real people act erratically.* Again, the point of a simulation is to focus on key relationships, not on the entire range of human behavior. People in real life might be distracted because their cat is lost, or they have to go to the bathroom, or they have a doctor's appointment. If "attention" is not one of the key variables being taught, it is taken out of the equation in a simulation, enabling people to learn more consistently and methodically.

These are all educational reasons for not opting for a multi-player simulation. Having said all of that, there are so many non-educational reasons, including competition, buzz, and sheer fun, that a fair number of educational simulation designers will choose to create experiences with multi-player components.

How Accurate Is Accurate Enough?

Another issue we had to deal with was the perpetual question: How accurate do simulations have to be to be valid teaching tools? Said more technically, to what degree does a simulation have to be predictive and/or of very high fidelity in order to be instructive?

As with other questions concerning realism in simulations, the answer to this question will change with time. Simulations will become increasingly realistic. But they will never perfectly replicate reality. How can I be sure? Because across time and technologies, once a simulation in a given area becomes perfect, you could take the person out of the equation altogether and just automate the system.

Simulations are there to help people, not replace them—or as General George S. Patton, Jr., once said, "All of this talk about super-weapons and push-button warfare is a pile of junk. Man is the only war machine. Man has to drive tanks, fly planes, crawl through the mud, pull the triggers, and push the buttons."

In fact, there are several reasons you might not want a simulation to perfectly reflect real life. For instance, the environment provided by a simulation may actually be a better one for learning than real-life situations, which almost always contain a fair number of distractions. The example that Stephen Alessi and Stanley Trollip give in *Computer-Based Instruction: Methods and Development* is a good one:

The cockpit of a modern airplane is one of the worst learning environments possible. Not only are there many instruments confronting the novice pilot but also constant messages being relayed to
and from the traffic controllers from all aircraft in the vicinity. . . .
the novice pilot is usually apprehensive about being up in the air
and is also concerned about other aircraft nearby. All this creates a
situation in which most attention is being concentrated on aspects
actually irrelevant to the immediate task at hand, which is learning
to control the plane. (p. 173)

Given that people are part of the equation, in simulation design, perfection is not always as perfect as you might hope. Part of
the goal of any simulation is to focus the end-learner on a finite, not
infinite, set of relationships. While the number of relationships will
grow both as simulations become more powerful and as we become
more used to learning from them, simulations will never reach the
infinite subtlety of life, nor should they.

One analogy is bird guides. Some guides use photographs of
birds, such as the *National Audubon Society Field Guide to North
American Birds*. These pictures are, by all standards, as accurate as
possible. They are nearly perfect.

Yet the lists of best-selling bird books are dominated by guides
using illustrations, such as the classic books by Roger Tory Peterson,
the recent best-selling *Sibley Guide to Birds* by David Sibley, Kauf-
man Focus Guides, *National Geographic Field Guide to the Birds of
North America*, and even the best-selling coffeetable book, *Birds*, by
Robert Bateman.

How can this be if accuracy is key? Clearly there are other issues. Illustrations provide an editorial ability of the expert both to
highlight certain aspects and to pull out some of the background.
Cooking books, carpentry manuals, and similar guides in fact use
carefully rendered illustrations rather than photographs, despite the
fact that illustrations are actually more expensive to produce.

When I asked the Sims franchise mastermind Will Wright about
accuracy, he said:

In most interesting fields, like weather modeling, predictive simulations are very difficult or impossible. However, the property of weather being unpredictable can be a property of a good educational simulation.

Let me give you an example. Say you put the ball on the tip of a cone, and let it go. A perfect *predictive* simulator would tell you exactly which side of the cone the ball would fall for the exact condition set-up. A *descriptive* simulator, like SimCity, would probably use a random variable to decide which side the ball would fall down. While that simulation would fail at being predictive, it would teach both the range of possibilities (that is, the ball never falls up), and also from a planning perspective, it teaches that you can't rely on predicting the exact outcome. You have to deal with the chaos and randomness. This might, ultimately, be even more realistic.

Television shows that are described as "realistic" provide the bar. No TV content is unedited, or un-editorialized. News programs are highly arranged. Even so-called "reality shows" are, in fact, thirty- to sixty-minute strings of edited pieces of tape showing only the "reality" the producers think is most dramatic, inspiring, or ridiculous. In fact, I believe reality shows follow the same formula as granola bars: The less granola that is actually in a granola bar, the better it tastes. Still, the formula doesn't work unless the audience is willing to suspend judgment and engage with the "content" presented. The creators have to earn our trust and be convincing, entertaining, and educational, and, well, accurate enough.

The Problem with Principles

When things are easy, being principled is easy. It is only when things get tough that principles matter. Keeping true to these principles would test all of our creative, analytical, and technical skill. And, most of all, it would test our will.

Chapter Eleven

The Beginning of Open-Ended Content

Sets and Figures

> The more creative the players can be, the more
> they like the simulation. There is nothing more
> satisfying than solving a problem in a unique way.
> Another aspect is being able to describe yourself to
> the game either directly or through your actions,
> and watching the game build around you.
> —*From a conversation with Will Wright,*
> *creator of SimCity and The Sims*

As with making a movie, we needed both sets and characters for Virtual Leader. Unlike a movie, the sets would be interactive—players would be able to move around in them at their own will. And the characters would end up, literally, having minds of their own.

Modeling Space: The Sets

What is the most boring place in the world? Right, a corporate meeting room. Beige walls, beige floors, beige tables, beige chairs. Everything has a faint shimmer of plastic. The trash bins always seem half-full (or half-empty, if you are an optimist). On whiteboards, there are faded red and blue scratches of diagrams from past meetings that were never completely erased. Three markers are strewn about, two of them are erasable, and one is permanent to tempt you to ruin the expensive whiteboard forever. Every problem in a meeting room seems detached and overly intellectual. These are places where people seem at their least interesting.

And we were going to have our entire simulation in these rooms. I'm serious.

To make things worse, we would have to make our meeting rooms even more generic, because the off-the-shelf version of the product was to depict a universal corporation, whatever that means.

Having said that, the meeting rooms could not be mere neutral sets. They actually had to accomplish quite a bit.

In most computer games, players gather more power as they progress. They get faster cars, a larger arsenal of weapons, or more money to spend at the virtual mall. They can build larger additions to their mansion or larger spaceships for their fleet. In Virtual Leader, the player starts as the most powerful person in the room. As a player becomes involved with bigger and bigger issues, he or she progressively becomes the person in the room with the least power. So the meeting rooms had to be the dominant clue, and reward, for the player's progress upward in the organization.

The meeting rooms, in a sense, had to be characters as well. They had to convey information about what was going on as much as any piece of dialogue. They had to bestow power on certain people. They had to set a tone.

And as with a sitcom set, the rooms had to be interesting. They had to be places to which people wanted to return five or ten or even twenty times as they replayed the experience. Because the players could use the arrow keys to move around the room, they had to have interesting pieces of information scattered around that were fun to find but not essential to the experience.

With those goals in mind, we began.

Meeting Room One

The Virtual Leader story begins with your first day on a new job. The first scenario is the only situation in which the player interacts with just one other character, so we used the opportunity to not have the set be a formal meeting room; instead, Meeting One takes place in a private office, the player/learner's (Figure 11.1).

Figure 11.1 Drawing and Rendering the Set for Meeting One

This allowed a bit more intimacy. The room had to be sparse, both to dovetail with the story, but also to minimize distractions as the player was learning how to use the controls for the first time.

We also wanted the shabbiness of the office to suggest that maybe the on-screen character was feeling that taking this job wasn't the best move after all. The player had to have mixed feelings about the boss to take into later meetings. This set also framed the company, called Nortic, not as some idealistic, perfect, perky environment, but one with gaping flaws. In other words, it was a company that needed leadership.

Meeting Room Two

The second leadership situation takes place in a break room (Figure 11.2). It is the gathering place for overworked, underpaid, resentful call center employees. These people are being impacted by deci-

Figure 11.2 Drawing and Rendering the Set for Meeting Two

sions that they cannot influence. We wanted the room to be dark and dingy, buried literally in the bowels of the company. This really set the bar so low that the player could rise significantly for each of the next three straight meetings.

In the break room, the plant was dead, the shades of green were terrible, and even the fluorescent bulbs were burned out. The garbage can overflowed. The only natural light came from a tiny window at ground level. (The amount of natural light and number of plants became our barometer for status, with the better environments having increasingly more of both).

Maybe we outdid ourselves. The break room really was terrible. If we had thought that the player would ever spend time looking at the entire room at once, we might have toned it down. We didn't want to really depress anyone, but, unfortunately, we didn't have the luxury of offering selected views. Because we spent a long time looking at the pictures of the room as we were writing dialogue, it actually began depressing us as well. What a terrible room!

On the plus side, as the players shifted their view around the room, they were "rewarded" with a lot of details that better explained why the situation was how it was. My Dickens side was also hoping that plenty of senior officers would engage the simulation. I wanted to make the point, not so subtly, that often enough the employees in the worse situations are the ones who have the most contact with customers.

Meeting Room Three

Meeting Three took place in my favorite room, the one that we would use in all of the brochures (Figure 11.3). Maybe this was just because it finally got us out of that terrible basement. The windows were huge, the trees and grass and sky were all appealing. The gold column in the corner added a nice design element. We didn't want to make the environment too nice, though, so we made the chairs and table cheaper.

Figure 11.3 Drawing and Rendering the Set for Meeting Three

This was also the room that was at about the organizational level of most of the people to whom we showed Virtual Leader. Most people "recognized" the room, and many even asked if it was based on a room from their organization.

Even though this set was so much better than Meeting Two, I still wanted it to suggest that the company had some major flaws. We put on the walls some of those moronic HR posters. One said, "Quality Is Impossible Without U," and another had an Orwellian quote, "Competition Is Security." Typical of a slightly interactive environment, these posters were not in the player's face. They were there to be found as the player looked around.

We could not do everything we had originally wanted. For example, we had envisioned a parking lot outside, full of cars visible through the glass walls of the meeting room. We ended up not being able to use the cars, because they would overwhelm some of the older graphic processors. They also looked static, just parked there. Maybe the next version.

Meeting Room Four

Meeting Five was to be the grand finale, set in a big, formal boardroom, so we had a bit of trouble coming up with a distinctive setting for Meeting Four (Figure 11.4). Most of our early renditions looked too much like either Three or Five.

Figure 11.4 Drawing and Rendering the Set for Meeting Four

Finally, someone suggested that the meeting could be held outside, at one of those plush corporate retreats. The inspiration came from a corporate retreat in Norwalk, Connecticut, now owned by Prudential. It had been a monastery, converted by a corporate consortium led by GTE.

This decision made sense for a lot of reasons. First, it would be as close to this level of luxury as some of the players would ever really get, so it seemed like a fun place to be. But also, it seemed like an appropriate and ironic place to be discussing major layoffs.

If the players wanted to look around, there were plenty of things to find. We put a white linen cloth on the table, topped off with fresh fruit and water. There is even a golf course up to the left, if you look hard enough.

Meeting Room Five

Everything in the Meeting Five set was done to convey as much formal authority and importance as possible (Figure 11.5). The rugs were oriental. The columns were marble. The paneling and furniture were rich walnut and burgundy leather. We also inserted some very modern elements, such as security cameras and panels that open to reveal a projector. It is in this room, at this moment, that the fate of the company is decided, and the player is part of it.

Figure 11.5 The Set for the Grand Finale

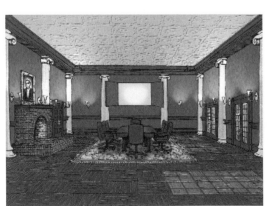

Figure 11.5 The Set for the Grand Finale, Cont'd

The picture above the fireplace was of SimuLearn co-founder Ken Kupersmith. We stole a picture and had it made into a painting without his knowing. By the time he realized, the graphics were locked and loaded. This picture is far off the left for those who were really looking around (although front and center in the screen shot shown in Figure 11.5).

The Characters

Because of budget and time restrictions, we could only have five characters other than the person the end-learner played. These characters had to traverse the corporate spectrum, from the lowest ranks to the highest. As with the sets, they had to be generic enough to be "every employee." While we knew we would have to add characters for custom implementations, we wanted a cast that could both be reused and not alienate potential corporate buyers.

But, as with the rooms, we couldn't make them too generic either. We couldn't just slap together five Lands' End models and try to pass them off as corporate employees. They couldn't be interchangeable. We had to give them personalities. We wanted them all to be thought of as real people, annoying in some ways and impressive in others. No one would be perfect. While most of their personalities would come later in their voices and dialogue, we needed to start with a firm, graphical foundation.

Oli

Oli was a call center employee, and our own version of a slacker (Figure 11.6). His clothing had to reflect a general sloppiness, but still be acceptable to corporate America. (Or almost acceptable. Several GE employees were appalled by Oli, stating accurately, and proudly, that he would never work there.). Those organizations that worked with unions assumed that Oli was the representative.

From a leadership perspective, he was also a character that would represent the outsider. He could come up with ideas that were creative, far from mainstream, but either he would not introduce them because he was under-powered, or his ideas would be shot down by the traditionalists.

Figure 11.6 Oli: The Person Everyone Loves to Hate

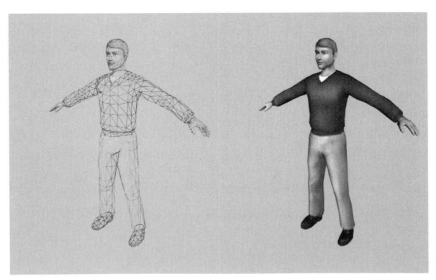

Rosa

Rosa is a constant voice of reason. We thought of her as the conservative HR professional, always trying to calm people down and do what is right. Rosa went through many iterations, starting harsher, more severe, and mellowing to a prettier and softer look, with lighter hair and a pink and blue outfit (Figure 11.7).

Figure 11.7 The Many Iterations of Rosa

Herman

We needed, in the words of Shakespeare scholars, a wise fool (Figure 11.8). We wanted someone to provide comic relief, who would come out with sarcastic one-liners. But we also needed this person to give the player critical pieces of information along with a healthy dose of cynicism. The players who would eventually engage the simulation the best learned to ask Herman for his opinion as often as possible to get "the real scoop."

Figure 11.8 Herman: The Wise Fool

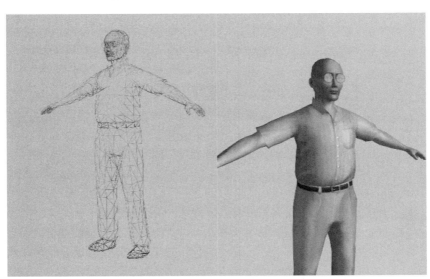

Will

Will is initially the player/learner's boss, and he is a flawed boss (Figure 11.9). We had to be careful both in how we designed him visually and in how we wrote him. We didn't want him to be over-the-top terrible, because that would be unrealistic and because many bosses would be asking their employees to play this. But we also had to, from a leadership perspective, underline some of the faults of over-use of formal authority.

Will is a star in Meeting Three, the one that would eventually be called our "Enron scenario." How do you work within the system to make minor corrections without resorting to either whistle-blowing or letting major mistakes happen?

Figure 11.9 Will: The Flawed Boss

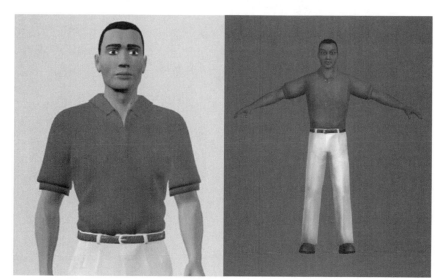

Alan

Alan represented our high-level authority figure (Figure 11.10). We borrowed ideas from President Bartlet from "The West Wing" and my one-time boss, Xerox Executive Vice President Wayland Hicks. Alan is strong, authoritative, formal, a master of classical knowledge. He also (unlike Wayland) likes to hear himself talk just a little too much.

Some people really had a problem with Alan. They thought he was condescending and arrogant. Others loved him and thought him almost fatherly, too quickly following him blindly. This level of interpretation made the simulation a powerful, Rorschach-like diagnostic experience, as well as a leadership trainer.

In a Jungian sense, we wanted all of our characters to represent archetypes as well as distinctive characters. This would become important later on, as corporate coach types who became early advocates of Virtual Leader would point to each character as an example of someone their clients actually knew.

Figure 11.10 Alan: Loves to Hear Himself Speak

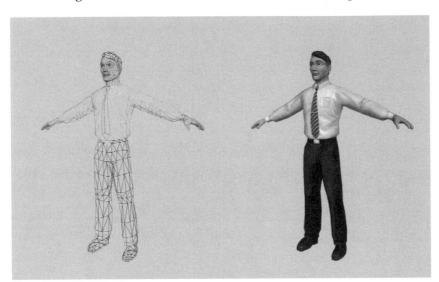

Adjusting Course

Computer graphics, like comic books and science fiction, tend toward the Wagnerian. They can be dramatic. They tend to be melodramatic. Characters tend to be overly defined. This is true not only of their personalities, but also of the way their physical characteristics are rendered.

And any time you deal with anatomy, you have to deal with delicate issues. Getting the balance right is tricky.

Our original Rosa was criticized by many as being built too much like video game superstar Lara Croft. ASTD's Pat Galagan looked at an early screen shot and commented that "the trees looked more natural than Rosa" (Figure 11.11).

We had to adjust certain properties to make her more acceptable to our target audience. We at least came close.

Other problems of anatomy were not so obvious at first. For example, Meeting One happens in a small office, a more intimate setting than the other situations. Every so often, if Oli got really

Figure 11.11 Rosa Had to Be Toned Down

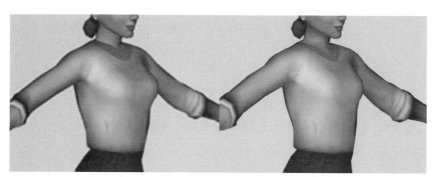

stressed, he had the habit of standing up. Further, because the screen did not automatically pan up to keep Oli's head at eye level (which was unnecessary in other meetings), the players might feel as if they were inappropriately staring just a bit too low on Oli's anatomy.

We had a few embarrassing situations when this happened. At one conference, when SimuLearn co-founder Tom Parkinson was showing a potential customer the Meeting One scenario with a crowd behind him, the awkward viewing angle seemed especially pronounced. So Tom smoothly pulled up the thought balloon, and used it to censor the shot appropriately (Figure 11.12).

Figure 11.12 A Good Save: When Oli Stood Up in Meeting One

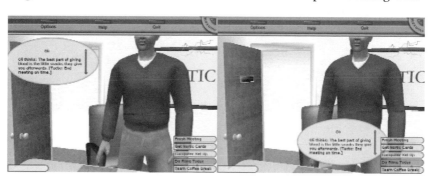

At this point the customer's face was beet red, and I was sure we had lost the sale. We made some quick changes to the code to prevent Oli from standing in Meeting One, and the problem was solved from then on. This kind of problem would never have happened with pure linear content!

The Edge of Linearity

Like branching videos, *models* and *sets* are just at the transition between linear and non-linear content, tending toward the linear side. It was a line we would soon have to cross into full-blown non-linearity.

Chapter Twelve

What Do People Do All Day?

The Animation System

The ON and OFF states of a simple flashlight are
different and therefore warrant a state network with
two distinct states.

—*Jonathan Kaye,*
FlashMX for Interactive Simulations

One of the easiest simulation calculation models is called state-based. It is even easier than branching. Here's how it was explained to me.

Imagine you have arrived at a Hilton Head resort. You start off in registration (Figure 12.1).

Figure 12.1 A Resort Example of a Simple-State-Based Model

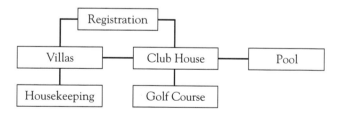

You first go to your villa to change out of your travel clothes. You might quickly check with housekeeping to find out what time they clean the rooms each day. Then you head out to the clubhouse, with your spouse going to the golf course and you heading to the pool. You agree to meet back at the clubhouse in two hours.

In this example, each location is a called a "state." It is a discrete place. The states are then connected selectively. You can go between the golf course and the clubhouse, but you cannot go directly to the golf course from registration.

As a simulation model, this approach has plenty of advantages. There is an open-ended feel to it in that you can go anywhere you want. You can backtrack. You can spend as long as you want in any given state.

This can be a model of exploration. There is a sense of freedom. There is no inherent time limit either. A person can stay in our resort forever.

There is some ability here for "play." You can make some links between states one-way. Or you can establish certain conditions for moving from one state to another. In our Hilton Head example, to extend the analogy, there could be a pass needed to get into the pool that is only available from housekeeping.

To stretch the analogy even further, imagine there is a really loud couple, let's call them Fran and John, whom you simply can't stand. Every time they see you they talk endlessly about their trip to Vietnam. You decide to avoid them at all costs. A state-based calculation model to simulate this dynamically restricted environment would give you complete access to everywhere but a location with Fran and John. You may want to get to the pool, but you can't go there until Fran and John leave the clubhouse.

State-Based Animation in Action

Using a state-based framework is hardly ever interesting enough as the primary calculation engine for a simulation. But its simplicity makes it very appropriate for many supporting parts of the simulation. We used it most extensively to control our animation, a critical part of our output system.

The Main Roles

The animation system in Virtual Leader was to constantly communicate how the character *felt* about the speaker and the idea and also how *tense* he or she was. Pierre-Henri Thiault, Virtual Leader's project manager, masterminded an elegant and powerful system to accomplish both functions. At any given time, the animation system would control:

- Turning the head of the bot toward whoever was speaking;
- Moving the lips according to what the bot was saying;
- Blinking and breathing;
- Controlling the facial animation; and
- Controlling the broad body animation.

These five animation tasks had to be done simultaneously as well as almost independently of each other. For example, a character could be shaking her head while looking up at the ceiling, blinking, and talking.

Animating Movement

Our system used skeletal animations. That is, the models we built of all of the characters had working parts. They had joints and bones. Our animations described the skeletal movements, and the skin just went along for the ride. The nice thing about this approach is that the same animations could be used on all of the bots. (Well, almost all of the bots. We actually had to use different animations for male and female bots.) The same animation gesture that made Oli shake his head in disgust controlled Alan's head shake as well. This made it very easy to change a small animation in one place and have it be changed in all bots, in all meetings.

For the sake of illustrating a state-based system in action, let's look just at the system that controls the broad-body movements.

The other systems worked in very much the same way. Pierre defined fifteen primary states, as follows:

A   Sitting up to table, distance normal

B   Standing up in front of chair

C   Sitting, leaning forward in chair

D   Sitting far from table

E   Sitting all the way back in chair

F   Sitting, leaning all the way forward

G   Slight leaning back, arms not crossed

H   Slight leaning back in chair, crossed arms

I   Leaning forward with pen in hand

J   Leaning forward with cup

K   Standing with cup

L   Standing behind chair

M   Standing with pen

N   Standing, arms crossed

O   Standing, leaning on arms

Each state had several animations associated with it. For standing up, as an example, we had listening, squirming, short cough, and longer cough.

Pierre also defined which states could transition to which other states (Figure 12.2). A bot could go from leaning forward to learning back in one turn, for example, but could not go from leaning forward to standing up or being behind a chair.

So for every connection, we also had to define a transition animation. These included picking up a pen (C to I), putting down a mug (J to C), or sitting down (B to A). As with airlines, we had hub animations and spoke animations, to minimize the number of connections.

Figure 12.2 Connections Between the Animation States

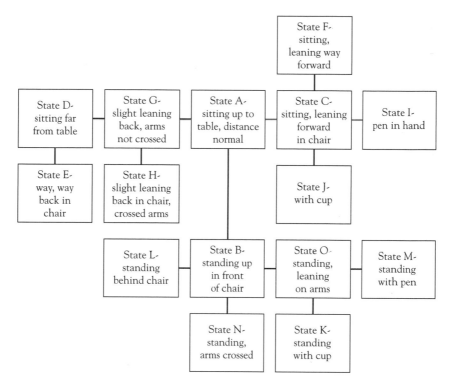

In our hypothetical resort game example, the player might control the movement between states. To traverse animation states in Virtual Leader, we had the program, not the learner/player, control the movement. For each state we defined an opinion and a tension description. Leaning all the way back in a chair, for example, depicted very low tension. Leaning forward, quickly clicking a pen represented very high tension. Leaning forward holding the cup, slowly rubbing it, depicted a productive tension and high approval. Standing up behind the chair represented dislike for the speaker or the idea.

Then we had the artificial intelligence system tell the animation system what the bot was feeling, and the animation system would shift the bot to the right state. In keeping with our desire for open-endedness, we had probabilities, not hard links, controlling this state shifting. If a bot leaning was nervous, there might be a 10 percent chance it picked up a pen and started tapping, a 30 percent chance that it would stand up, and a 60 percent chance it would stay in the same place. This kept the animations from becoming predictable, although it made the system hard to debug.

"Do you realize," Pierre asked me late night, his office wall filled with sketches, "that we will be presenting more information than a week-long course on body-language, and that's not even the point of the simulation?"

A Smart Graphic Engine

Animations are controlled by *graphic engines*, one of the most expensive and time-consuming parts of building a simulation. We decided to build our own.

Adopting a third-party graphics engine is a fast way to start, but, for example, a graphics engine built for the gaming industry is buying into a specific genre. Jon Blossom and Collette Michaud wrote a warning about their use of game engines in their account of building a product for their educational simulation, aimed at teaching physics to teenagers:

> Ironically, the choice to use the Jedi Knight engine rather than rolling our own 3D world simulation system proved to be one of the worst problems we had to face.
>
> In choosing the Jedi engine, we hoped to benefit from its physics simulator as much as from its rendering engine. We wanted our game to teach simple physics in an open-ended environment, and we hoped concepts of velocity, acceleration, and gravity would just fall out of the simulator. How wrong could we have been! . . . The physics engine had been tuned to make maximum fun out of running characters and flying projectiles. We had hoped to teach interactive real-world physics, not cartoon game physics in which the

main character could run 80 miles an hour, nothing bounced, and nothing could be pushed!

We decided it was worth it to build our own to avoid this kind of genre resurgence. While expensive and time-consuming, in no small part due to the talent of our programmers, we made the right choice.

One important part of a graphics engine, and an integral part of ours, is the ability to intelligently fill in, or smooth, the transition between two different animations. We had a glitch where the mug in a bot's hand was accidentally defined as being very large in one animation set. Our graphics engine was smart enough to compare the two mug sizes and smoothly show the mug growing to epic proportions, rather than having it just suddenly appear huge. Pierre's team had done such a great job with the graphics engine that it could blend animations together, therefore potentially creating unlimited numbers of movements that could be generated on the fly.

Fine-Tuning

In keeping with another of our core beliefs, we designed the animation system to be highly flexible. We could control how often, and if at all, certain animations were triggered.

This meant that when we first finished the program, the animation system was not tuned well at all. The bots would stand up, then sit down, then lean forward, then lean back. They were exhausting to watch. They all looked as if they had just had about six double lattes. We calmed all the characters down considerably.

There were some animations that were great, but we just couldn't use them anywhere. One was "the wave." The original idea was that if a bot were bored, he or she would wave to someone outside of the meeting room. As it turned out, the wave looked as if the bot was waving to the person across the table. The effect was just bizarre.

Another animation we created but didn't use was a thumbs up. It was meant to be an approval animation. But it never looked right, and we eventually just set its probability of happening down to zero.

Some animations didn't come out the way we hoped, no matter how hard we tried. This was especially true of tight facial expressions. One broad smile looked like a grimace. We tinkered and tinkered, but never got it right. So we just renamed it "grimace," changed the activation logic from happy and relaxed to unhappy and tense, and called it a day.

There were other gestures that were met with mixed reaction from the corporate community. If the bots get really mad, for example, they might bang their fists on the table. There is a great booming sound that goes with it, and it tends to get everyone's attention. Some cultures never show disapproval this way and hate this animation. Others never do it this way and love this animation. And some do it this way routinely (especially the Wall Street people) and don't look at it twice.

What a Simulation Teaches

We did not set out to teach awareness of body language. That was not our original intent within our scope of leadership. But Pierre did such a thorough job that it has become a major selling point. People leave with experience highly focused on information they never registered before.

Although we pushed the boundaries, the animation system was an evolution of a system that had been used in computer games. With the dialogue system we were going deeper into the unknown. And for the first time, we realized we might have gone too far.

Chapter Thirteen

The Ultimate Hurdle

The Dialogue System

> Our language is taken to be the key ingredient of
> our possession of consciousness.
>   —*Roger Penrose,* The Emperor's New Mind

If you and I talk, the conversation is dynamic. We can agree quickly, or we can debate. We can bring up different topics. We can conclude an idea. We can agree not to pursue an idea. We can switch back and forth. We can compliment each other or take jabs.

Conversations in movies and television shows are, of course, linear. The writers carefully construct every last utterance. One character says something, and the other character can deliver the perfect response.

Computer games are pioneers of interactivity. Yet when it comes to dialogue, when real actors' voices are used, most computer games are pretty conservative. They use one or some combination of four types of basically linear dialogue systems:

1. In a typical game, the player battles or races or flies or plots through some highly interactive scenario and, after winning, leans back and watches characters talking to each other to set up the next highly interactive scenario. These *cut-scenes* are direct counterparts to the Hollywood style of writing.

2. Some games use short *branching dialogue trees*. A character talks to you, and you are given three possible responses. Depending on your response, the other character will say one of several different sound bites, or maybe even dive for cover.

3. Some games, as in Deus Ex, also insert different dialogue in situations in response to some of your actions. You are playing a male character; if you wander into the women's bathroom when exploring the corporate headquarters, your boss, two scenes later, will reprimand you (not that I have ever done this, I hasten to add. I have just heard this to be true).

4. A more advanced type of system uses different dialogue categories to signal changes of states in onscreen characters. In the game Thief, for example, you sneak around large castles trying not to be noticed. If the guards don't suspect you are there, they will say things like, "Sure is cold tonight. I should have brought something warmer" or "What a quiet night." If you knock something over or make noise running across a hard surface, the guard goes into alert mode and might say something like, "I heard you" or "Who's that?" Finally, if the guard can't find you, he will return to a bored state and might say, "I guess it was my imagination" or "Must be a rat." If he does find you, the guard goes into attack mode, and he might say, "Say your prayers, thief," "I need some help over here," or "This is the last house you will ever rob."

This last system was closest to what we wanted to use. I convinced Ken, who was responsible for watching the money, that with this as a model, it would be that easy to create a satisfactory dialogue system.

Supporting and Opposing Dialogue

The four primary states that we would represent were the characters'

- Supporting an idea,
- Opposing an idea,
- Supporting a person, and
- Opposing a person.

For each state, we established a bucket of quotes, from which the program would draw one randomly. So instead of "Must be a rat," we would use something more like, "It makes sense to me" or

"You seem to know what you're talking about. What do you think?" We built up a library of generic quotes, applicable to virtually all of the people and all of the ideas we would be discussing.

Creating non-linear anything, especially dialogue, is as precise as any computer programming. You have to write lines without knowing what is going to come before or after them. You wouldn't want a situation, for example, where one person supports an idea by saying, "I will provide the funding," and the next person says, "We don't have any money for it." We had to broadly define reasons for or against arguments, and use them consistently. Lack of money was always used against an idea. The skill and dedication of the team was always used as a reason to favor or support an idea.

The specific tense and sentence structure became very important as well, as we never knew exactly the context for any given quote. For example, if a character were to support a given idea, she should not say, "I agree," because, for all we knew, the person before her might have said, "This is the stupidest thing I ever heard." Instead, she would have to say, "I agree with the idea."

I mapped out the high-level dialogue structure. Every quote was expensive, both in terms of paying the talent to record them, and in terms of taking up space on the program, so I had to use as few as possible. We would have seven characters (the five staple characters plus a male and female version of the player's voice), each with fifteen quotes (for variety) in each of the 4 buckets. That would be 420 quotes we needed to write, record, and store for Virtual Leader.

"That seems reasonable," Ken said. He drummed his fingers. "If you find that we need to go a little higher than the 420 number, maybe add ten or twenty more, feel free to do it. We need to get this right."

"I don't think we will need to," I said. "This should cover everything."

Separating Ideas into Plans and Premises

My team began mapping our situations into dialogue buckets. I realized with some discomfort that the general category of "idea" did not fit enough of our leadership issues. We realized we had to break up ideas into *premises* and *plans*. Premises were ideas that could be debated ("We should make our mascot be a red cat with one eye"), and plans were things where the conversation revolved around how to complete the work in the future ("How can we create a customer survey?").

What is interesting is that while opposing a premise seems straightforward ("We tried that last year and it didn't work"), the way you oppose work in our model was to prolong it ("We should do more research"). Once I recognized that, I saw this technique used all the time by politicians, both inside the beltway and in corporations, as covert opposition. So many groups assume that studying a problem will bring them closer to a solution, when so often it has the opposite effect of consuming vast resources without producing anything.

Generic Plan Quotes

We wanted the bots to be able to change their minds during the course of a meeting. So it was critical not to have any opinion be too emphatic, allowing people the intellectual opportunity to change their minds without having to acknowledge it in the context of the meeting (Exhibit 13.1).

Exhibit 13.1 Generic Plan Quote Buckets and Examples

plan-neg	plan-pos
I don't know why this keeps coming up. It just does not seem feasible.	I am available before 6 A.M. Wednesday for follow-up.
I don't like the haphazardness of this plan.	I am very excited.
I don't like the sound of where this is going.	I bet we'll have a lot done by Monday.
I don't think I could line up enough experts in time.	I can book any conference room we may need.
I don't think I could line up enough help in time.	I can bring in some paint if we want to all pitch in.
	I love this kind of problem.

Generic Premise Quotes

We played hard with premise dialogue. We found that, rather than centering on a high philosophical debate, the dialogue worked better around doing a specific action. (Exhibit 13.2). This might be, "We should meet after the teleconference" or "Let's spend the money on improving customer retention."

Exhibit 13.2 Generic Premise Buckets and Examples

prem-neg	prem-ntrl	prem-pos
I am not so sure about it.	I'm leaning one way, but I really don't know.	As I go through all of the variables, I haven't hit a hard stop yet.
I am not sure it is a good idea.	Doing it makes sense. Not doing it makes sense.	The idea makes a lot of sense.
I am still too uncomfortable with this.	Honestly, I am leaning one way, but only slightly.	I don't see anything holding us back.
I am leaning against doing it right now.	There are just not enough facts to resolve this yet.	The idea sounds good.
This won't turn out the way you want it to.	We might want more information before we can go ahead.	
There may be other priorities.		

By splitting up idea quotes into premises and plans, we had just added 210 more quotes to the original 420. Ken wasn't thrilled.

"630 quotes seem like a whole lot."

"I know."

He asked, "You couldn't cut it to, say, 500? Or 450?"

"It would make a lot more sense if we had all 630 of them."
Ken shook his head and made some notes. "Fine."

Custom Quotes

The supporting and opposing dialogue was beginning to work. It defined very clearly on which side a given bot was. It made clear how the opinion of the group was flowing. But it was, after all, generic. And because we used so much of it, it became a little numbing hearing the same types of phrases bandied back and forth:

Player [Re: Will's Sales Retreat]: I will work late tonight. STATE_POSITIVELY_ON_PLAN

Rosa [Re: Will's Sales Retreat]: It seems quite difficult. STATE_NEGATIVELY_ON_PLAN

Will [Re: Will's Sales Retreat]: We can't do it in the given time frame. STATE_NEGATIVELY_ON_PLAN

Maybe, just maybe, we were beginning to think, we would have to introduce "custom" quotes. A specific person, about a specific idea, in a specific meeting, would *trigger* these sound bites. Each quote would be used *once* during the entire simulation.

I did the math. We had five scenes. Each scene on average would have five characters (including a male and female option for the player) each talking about eight ideas. We would need two quotes *supporting* and two quotes *opposing* each idea. I scrawled on a piece of scrap paper, "$5 \times 5 \times 8 \times 4 = 800$ (+ 630 generic)."

"1430 quotes are it, right?" Ken said, that evening. "It's twice as high as it should be, but that will be as many as we need to go, right?"

"I think so," I said sheepishly. It turned out I was wrong.

Introductions and Conclusions

I had my friends running through all of my sample dialogue. I came to another conclusion. We had to add special custom quote buckets for when an idea was introduced for the first time. For example:

Will [Re: Will's Sales Retreat]: We need to start thinking about the annual customer appreciation bash. We are starting a little late this year, so I will need a lot of help to organize and recruit the perfect event committee. INTRODUCE_IDEA

That added 200 quotes. And after that we created special quotes to signal when the idea was finished:

Alan [Re: Low-Cost Provider]: Imagine our customers' surprise when we lower our prices every year instead of raise them. Transition is never easy though, even if it's for the better. What problem can we address next? WRAP_PLAN

These also had to be custom to the idea. That was another 200 quotes.

We then decided to put in negative introductions (200 to be exact) to go along with our positive introductions. These are ways of bringing up an idea without associating it with you personally (another favorite technique of politicians). Here, Herman raises an idea, while maintaining a distance from it:

Herman [Re: Move to States]: I hope we are not going to hear more of the tired old argument to relocate the facility back to the States. INTRODUCE_IDEA_NEG

Interpersonal Dialogue

Another type of dialogue was interpersonal dialogue. Its purpose was to establish a relationship and also to invite the target to take part in the discussion. This was easier for the positive and neutral comments. It was harder for negative comments, in that one both has to insult someone and ask him or her to talk.

Addressing Active and Passive Characters

In the same way we split the ideas into premises and plans, we were beginning to understand we had to split the people into two categories. If they had recently spoken, they were considered *active* characters. If they had not, they were considered *passive* characters. Exhibits 13.3 and 13.4 show examples of negative, neutral, and positive interpersonal dialogue for active and passive characters respectively. That added 210 more quotes. It was time to see Ken again.

Exhibit 13.3 Interpersonal Dialogue Addressing Active Characters

act-neg	*act-ntrl*	*act-pos*
Did you think of that all by yourself? If so, what else do you have? I am not sold yet by a long shot. Don't just create carbon dioxide. Sell me. I hear you but you are not making sense. Keep going.	Can you elaborate? Is it a good idea? Is there enough information? So, what else do you think about that? So, what's your opinion? We'd all like to hear what else you think. Well? Any thoughts? What do you think? Will you weigh in on this? You look like you have something else to add.	I find your comments to be quite insightful. What else? I really appreciate your effort. Keep going. I think you really get it. What else should we be thinking about? Keep going. You are on a roll. Keep up the good work. My initial opinion of you was wrong. I like you. What are you thinking about now?

Exhibit 13.4 Interpersonal Dialogue Addressing Passive Characters

pass-neg	pass-ntrl	pass-pos
Do you have an opinion on this yet?	Can I get your input on this?	And what do you think?
Have you formed any opinion yet? Any at all?	Care to share your thoughts?	Do you see any problems with this?
Have you formed your opinion yet?	Do you have anything to add?	Do you think this will work?
I really wish you would let me know what's on your mind.	I really need you to weigh in on this.	Do you think we are on the right track?
Not joining in may work some places but not here.	We need you to weigh in on this.	Have you formed an opinion yet? If so, tell me.
Sooner or later, 'you' have to make a decision.	We really need you to weigh in on this.	I can't know what you want unless you tell me.
We haven't heard anything from you. What about it?	What do you think about this?	If you want me to do something else, let me know.
You've been managing to keep secrets. What's on your mind, or am I assuming too much?	What do you think?	So, what's your opinion?
	What's on your mind?	Well? Any thoughts?
	Will you share your thoughts?	Would you share what you are thinking?
	You look like you have something to add.	You are very quiet. What's on your mind?
	Your opinion is really needed here.	

Other Additions

We then found we had to add a few more buckets of quotes to round out the whole experience.

Reintroduction Quotes

We had learned it was critical to introduce every idea with a custom quote. Every time we did not, the players had understandable confusion about what was being talked about. But when a conversation went a different way and returned to an earlier idea, we had to use generic quotes to reintroduce it (Exhibit 13.5). This is a bit unsatisfying when you just heard (or read) the conversation, but it worked well when the dialogue was accompanied by the visual cue of having the old idea fade and the new idea light up (105 new quotes).

Exhibit 13.5 Sample Reintroduction Quotes

reint-neg	reint-ntrl	reint-pos
A quick question. Can anyone still support this? Before we continue, have we given up on this yet? I am looking over my notes. Can anyone still support this? Someone is going to bring up this bonehead idea again, so I might as well bring it up first.	Hmmm. Now is a good time to resolve this. Now that I think about it, let's go back to this earlier issue. You know, what about this?	Actually, let's go back to this earlier issue Actually, we haven't finished discussing this yet. We never reached a solution for this one. Actually, we should return to this. Actually, we still have more work to do on this idea.

Segues

Finally, we needed some other buckets of segues just to smooth out the dialogue (Exhibit 13.6).

Exhibit 13.6 Examples of Segue Quotes

tran	wrap-end	move-on
At the risk of seeming erratic, there's something I want to bring up. You just triggered a thought. You know, there is something I want to bring up.	All right, let's be careful out there. Great meeting! Thanks for your input! It looks like we plowed through our agenda today! Thanks everyone. Wow, great meeting. I think we're done.	We don't need to go further with this. What should we tackle next?

We ended up with twenty-four different buckets of quotes (Exhibit 13.7) that fit together rigorously.

Exhibit 13.7 Virtual Leader's Quote Buckets

Focus	Quote Bucket	Description
People Directed	Act-neg Act-neut Act-pos	Expressing approval or disapproval to a character who has recently spoken, and increases the chance that they will speak next.
	Pass-neg Pass-neut Pass-pos	Hands microphone over to a passive (hasn't spoken in a while) participant while expressing approval or disapproval.
Idea Directed	Int-end-neg** Int-end-pos**	Introduces the end of the meeting, which is treated as a premise.
	Int-neg** Int-neut** Int-pos**	Introduces an idea (premise or plan) for the first time. It is almost always a custom quote. Should be followed by a custom quote. Use a trans statement before it to transition from a previously discussed idea.
	Move-on	Acknowledges that support of an idea has collapsed. Replaces a pass-neg or prem-neg for the final finishing/stopping of an idea.
	Plan-neg* Plan-pos*	Contributes either support or opposition to a plan already introduced and active.
	Prem-neg* Prem-neut Prem-pos*	Contributes thoughts to a premise already introduced and active.
	Reint-neg Reint-neut Reint-pos	Reintroduces an idea that has already been introduced but is no longer the active idea. Should be followed by a custom quote.
	Tran	In the middle of an idea, table it, and set up the intro of another idea.
	Wrap-end** Wrap-plan** Wrap-prem**	Actual ending to meeting Close a plan idea (final). Mostly it will be custom. Close a premise idea (final). Mostly it will be custom.
* custom quotes available ** only custom quotes are used		

To fill out the database for the six characters in five situations, I proposed over *three thousand* lines of dialogue (Figure 13.1). I was soon back with Ken.

He looked through the buckets. He read all of the sample dialogue. Sometimes he nodded, other times he shook his head.

The clock ticked by. As he remained silent, I tried once again to see what could be taken out. But everything seemed necessary.

Ken paced. He sat down, and then stood up again. Finally he said, "This is obviously more than I had thought."

"I know," I replied.

"I can't say I am thrilled. I really wish there was another way." He cut himself off. He started to say something else, than stopped. I almost said something, but bit my tongue.

"I see where you are going with it. If you are sure this will work, if you are sure that this will be a stand-out feature of the simulation, if it will impress buyers, than I think we should do it."

"It will be very powerful, and people will be impressed," I said. We agreed to the plan. Luckily for the team's morale, it would take almost a year for me to find out that I was wrong again.

Meanwhile, I was not supposed to actually write much dialogue myself. My role was to set up the right template and let some other people fill in the three thousand holes. Unfortunately, the task of writing non-linear dialogue turned out to be much harder than anyone, especially I, imagined.

I was informed by my co-workers that I approached the task with a bit of a bad attitude. I just wanted to get it over as fast as possible, which already didn't seem that fast.

As I started working, however, I was reminded again of a basic simulation truth. Everywhere, every datum point, is a potential to add value.

I had originally looked at the dialogue system as a necessary evil, a low-impact tool to advance the action. As I started writing, I realized how much could be accomplished.

Figure 13.1 State Chart of Dialogue System

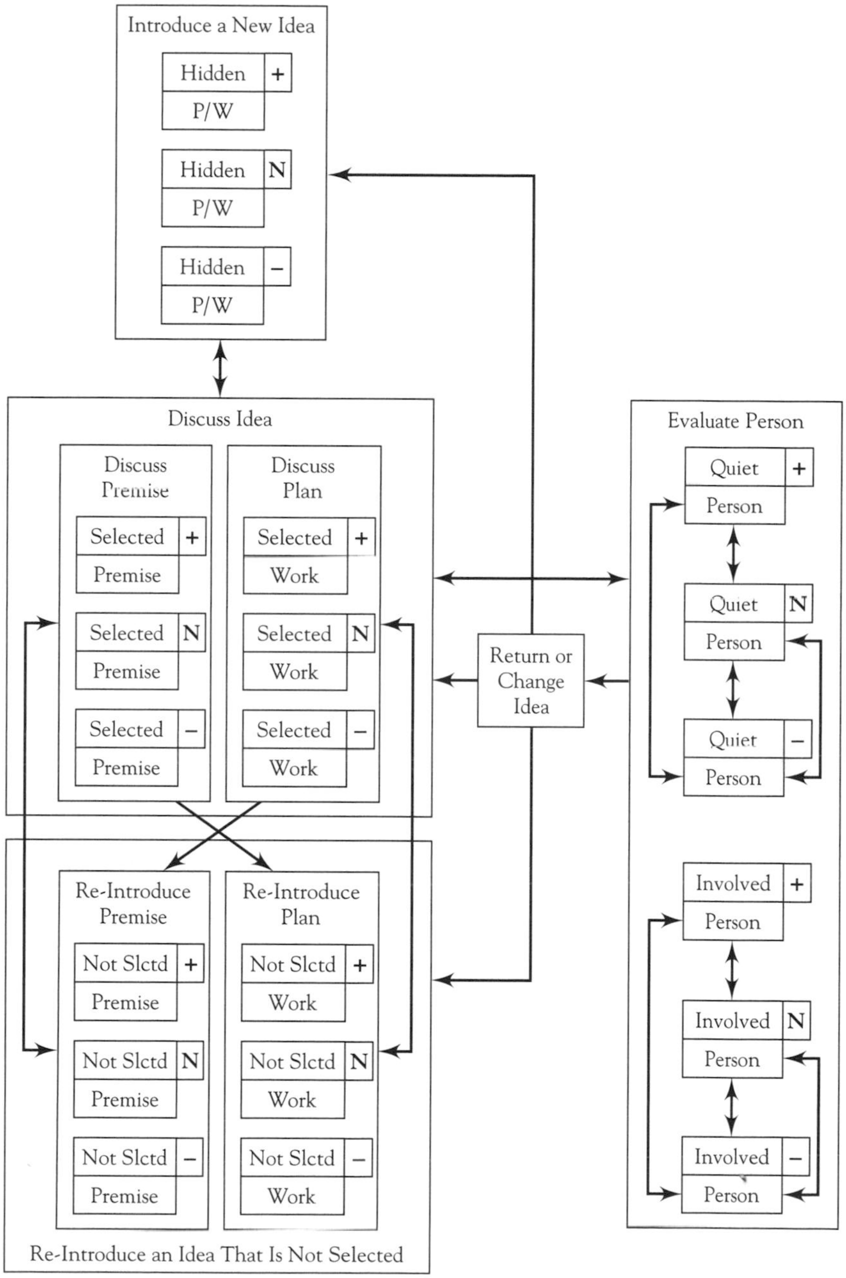

I could define characters. I could make some characters sarcastic and others earnest. I could write some amusing lines:

Herman: I've seen you support one bad idea after another. I have to admire your consistency though.

Rosa: Does anyone else think that an office party is an oxymoron? They're always more work than fun.

And of course I could always write Alan as "over the top."

Alan: Driving down the costs has the added benefit of helping the nation fight inflation.

Alan: I am impatient to begin the integration, but I sometimes remind myself to slow down by thinking of *The Book of Five Rings:* "If one tries to wield the long sword too quickly, he will become unable to wield it freely. To handle the long sword properly, it is essential to handle it calmly."

I could also role model some debates about big ideas. I could put in some inspirational and editorial comments.

Alan: Age will not be a criterion for downsizing. I have known too many sixty-year-olds whose greatest accomplishments were still ahead of them.

Rosa: Playing nice would not get to the real problems.

Oli: Some could say we are empowered. I think we are forgotten.

We also wanted to use some "strong" language, without offending anyone. We ended up with this:

Oli: The system is whacked!

And my all-time favorite ironic line:

Rosa: I will work on it Wednesday, instead of going to training.

Sample Virtual Leader Dialogues

When everything comes together, the effect is like this:

Meeting Three

In this scene, five characters are sitting around a meeting table. Will is your boss, and the senior person at the table. He is pushing hard for his idea of planning a big meeting. Other characters will introduce new ideas, but Will continues to bring everybody back to his focus. Once Will passes his idea, the group begins more serious discussions of other ideas.

The critical point is that the dialogue is spontaneous. It should flow despite the fact that it is dynamically generated and at any moment could go down a different path.

> *Will* [Re: Will's Sales Retreat]: We need to start thinking about the annual customer appreciation bash. We are starting a little late this year, so I will need a lot of help to organize and recruit the perfect event committee. INTRODUCE_IDEA_POSITIVELY

> *Player* [Re: Will's Sales Retreat]: You can use our customer database to add to the invitation list. STATE_POSITIVELY_ON_PLAN

> *Rosa* [Re: Will's Sales Retreat]: I've already been getting calls about it! I will circulate a list to get suggestions for the keynote speaker. STATE_POSITIVELY_ON_PLAN

> *Will* [Re: Will's Sales Retreat]: With everyone's help, and only with everyone's help, it's doable. STATE_POSITIVELY_ON_PLAN

> *Player* [to Will]: I think you really get it. What else should I be thinking about? STATE_POSITIVELY_ABOUT_AN_ACTIVE_NPC

Herman [Re: Will's Sales Retreat]: I volunteer to roll the red carpet out for Will wherever he goes. And fan him so he doesn't sweat. STATE_POSITIVELY_ON_PLAN

Will [Re: Will's Sales Retreat]: This couldn't come at a better time. It is always a great re-invigorator, and I will make it my top priority to make it happen. STATE_POSITIVELY_ON_PLAN

Rosa [Re: Will's Sales Retreat]: Why don't we break into two groups and meet later. STATE_POSITIVELY_ON_PLAN

Oli [Re: Will's Sales Retreat]: I think we have the right team for the job. STATE_POSITIVELY_ON_PLAN

Player [Re: Cut Expenses]: Actually, there is something I need to bring up. Should we tuck a bit of budget away for next quarter? People are saying this quarter's results will be really bad. TRANSITION, INTRODUCE_IDEA_POSITIVELY

Oli [Re: Will's Sales Retreat]: Now that I think about it, let's go back to this issue. REINTRODUCE_IDEA_POSITIVELY

Rosa [Re: Will's Sales Retreat]: If we spend the rest of the day brainstorming I think we can get it done. STATE_POSITIVELY_ON_PLAN

Player [Re: Will's Sales Retreat]: The project management will be difficult. STATE_NEGATIVELY_ON_PLAN

Herman [Re: Will's Sales Retreat]: We are in good shape. This will work well. STATE_POSITIVELY_ON_PLAN

Player [Re: Will's Sales Retreat]: Everyone I know is really stressed right now. They'll be into it, but not able to put in the hours. STATE_NEGATIVELY_ON_PLAN

Herman [Re: Will's Sales Retreat]: I will ask the senior officers to be on the steering committee, as long as they don't actually have to do anything. STATE_POSITIVELY_ON_PLAN

Will [Re: Will's Sales Retreat]: I'm very interested in getting your thoughts on this. Why don't Rosa and I sketch out a tentative agenda, and we'll see if we can put together a program that makes sense to everyone. What problem can we address next? WRAP_PLAN

Player [Re: Cut Expenses]: Now that I think about it, let's go back to this issue. REINTRODUCE_IDEA_POSITIVELY

Oli [to Rosa]: What are your thoughts so far? STATE_ POSITIVELY_ABOUT_AN_PASSIVE_NPC

Will [Re: Minutes on Website]: At the risk of seeming erratic, I have something I would like to bring up. Rosa, why don't you create a department website. That way we can post the minutes of our meetings. Can you make sure they get a hard copy of the status report upstairs? But be sure to sign off on it. TRANSITION, INTRODUCE_IDEA_POSITIVELY

Will [Re: Minutes on Website]: It's important that the people upstairs know what we're doing and Rosa has the knack for it. STATE_POSITIVELY_ON_PREMISE

Oli [Re: Go to Party]: You know, there is something I want to bring up. Today is Jonathan's last day. There's a little gathering for him over at R.J. Julia's. Shall we all head over there together after work? Say five thirty? TRANSITION, INTRODUCE_IDEA_POSITIVELY

Herman [Re: Go to Party]: It seems "sound" to me. STATE_POSITIVELY_ON_PREMISE

Player [Re: Go to Party]: If we do go together, we could go out for dinner afterward, if it's not too late. STATE_ POSITIVELY_ON_PREMISE

Player [to Herman]: I really appreciate your effort. Keep going. STATE_POSITIVELY_ABOUT_AN_ACTIVE_NPC

Herman [Re: Go to Party]: Parties are so much more tolerable as a group. Besides, my reputation is secure enough to be seen with all of you. STATE_POSITIVELY_ON_PREMISE

Here is another example of dialogue, between just two characters. This is part of the first scene, where the player is a new manager meeting with legacy employee Oli. Corey and Oli have different goals for the outcome of the meeting.

Meeting One

Oli [Re: Do Filing Today]: I finally put aside some time to do Rosa's filing. Can I do that and get back to you tomorrow afternoon? INTRODUCE_IDEA_POSITIVELY

Player [Re: Computer Set-Up]: Excuse me for interrupting, but there is something that is on my mind. Oli, can I ask you to help me get my computer set up right away? I'm at a loss without e-mail! I am sure you had other things planned, but can you make that happen? TRANSITION, INTRODUCE_IDEA_POSITIVELY

Oli [to Player]: I need a lot more information. STATE_NEGATIVELY_ABOUT_AN_ACTIVE_NPC

Player [Re: Computer Set-Up]: I can move around my schedule if that will avoid any other hold-ups. STATE_POSITIVELY_ON_PREMISE

Oli [Re: Finish Meeting]: Those are good thoughts. Let's switch gears for a minute though. There is a blood drive that is going on upstairs that will close up pretty soon. But I don't think that is a priority right now. TRANSITION, INTRODUCE_END_IDEA_NEGATIVELY

Player [Re: Computer Set-Up]: Now that I think about it, let's go back to this issue. REINTRODUCE_IDEA_POSITIVELY

Player [Re: Computer Set-Up]: The idea seems reasonable enough to me. STATE_POSITIVELY_ON_PREMISE

Player [Re: Computer Set-Up]: I really appreciate your help, Oli. Sorry I had to interrupt what you were doing. What else can we do? WRAP_PREMISE

Oli [Re: Finish Meeting]: Actually, we never reached a solution for this one. REINTRODUCE_IDEA_POSITIVELY

Player [Re: Finish Meeting]: Too many people could be rubbed the wrong way. STATE_NEGATIVELY_ON_PREMISE

Player [Re: Finish Meeting]: It doesn't seem like the best option. STATE_NEGATIVELY_ON_PREMISE

Player [Re: Get Nortic Cards]: That reminds me of something. Oli, Will says that you're the one to process business cards. I want to play up our group to the rest of Nortic as soon as possible. I know how busy you are, but does it make sense to get that ball rolling today? TRANSITION, INTRODUCE_IDEA_POSITIVELY

Oli [Re: Get Nortic Cards]: Are you really in a big hurry? You may not even need them a month from now. STATE_NEGATIVELY_ON_PREMISE

Player [Re: Get Nortic Cards]: I don't see how it could go wrong, as long as we can work through some little complaints. STATE_POSITIVELY_ON_PREMISE

Player [Re: Get Nortic Cards]: It seems pretty clear that we should do it. STATE_POSITIVELY_ON_PREMISE

Player [Re: Get Nortic Cards]: Can we prioritize this over your other obligations for today? STATE_POSITIVELY_ON_PREMISE

Oli [Re: Get Nortic Cards]: I can do it, but it might get Rosa a little irked. STATE_POSITIVELY_ON_PREMISE

Player [Re: Get Nortic Cards]: It seems like the right time.
STATE_POSITIVELY_ON_PREMISE

Oli [Re: Get Nortic Cards]: I don't have a problem with it.
STATE_POSITIVELY_ON_PREMISE

Oli [Re: Get Nortic Cards]: There are issues, sure. But I love
this kind of problem. STATE_POSITIVELY_ON_PREMISE

Oli [Re: Get Nortic Cards]: There goes the weekend.
STATE_POSITIVELY_ON_PREMISE

Oli [Re: Get Nortic Cards]: It seems like the right time.
STATE_POSITIVELY_ON_PREMISE

Player [Re: Get Nortic Cards]: Thank you so much, Oli. That
will be a big help. Any other big issues? WRAP_PREMISE

Oli [Re: Finish Meeting]: Hmmm. What about this?
REINTRODUCE_IDEA_NEUTRALLY

Player [Re: Finish Meeting]: I am trying to think of all of
the issues. But at this time I would have to say yes.
STATE_POSITIVELY_ON_PREMISE

Oli [Re: Finish Meeting]: The idea seems reasonable to me.
STATE_POSITIVELY_ON_PREMISE

Player [Re: Finish Meeting]: Looks like our time's up for now.
Thanks. WRAP_END

The Weakest Link?

One of the core features of Virtual Leader's dialogue system is its
ability to be modded (or modified). If an organization does not like
a particular line, they can just delete it outright. Virtual Leader will
automatically compensate for the line not being there. Or if an organization wants to add some dialogue, Virtual Leader will automatically cycle it in and play it at the right time.

Still, our dialogue remains the single area where we receive the most criticism. The thoughts fall in two categories:

- Some people want to choose the exact words they use. They want to construct the exact phrases or pick them from a list.
- Others point out that the dialogue sounds unnatural. Sometimes two characters will say the same thing, one after another. The first few times people play a scene they want more custom quotes.

I agree with both complaints. Part of our challenge is not just to reset expectations to prefer an interactive environment over a linear one, and not just to stress real-time interactivity, but also to keep the audience focused on the learning objectives.

Commented Bloomsburg University's Professor Karl Kapp, "Ultimately, the dialogue in the game is a convention that the learner has to become familiar with. Like in a shooter game where a well-known convention is that it takes more than one shot to kill you [the player], we all know that, in reality, that is probably not the case, but we tolerate this departure from reality so we can play the game without restarting all the time. In [Virtual Leader], dialogue is the major convention. Two people might not say the exact same thing one right after another in a meeting in reality, but the dialogue is a convention that holds meaning that is deeper than the words that are spoken."

The point of Virtual Leader is not to say the right thing. It is to *focus the conversation the right way*. In the same way, we didn't want people to focus too carefully on *what* was said, but instead on *why* it was said.

A Different Simulation?

Building a simulation that focuses on saying the perfect thing, say given a goal of bringing in someone who has been quiet, would be a valid, but different sort of endeavor. Trying to build a simulation that accomplished both would accomplish neither. It would defeat any game engine and break up the cyclical learning.

A paradox for Virtual Leader is that the better the dialogue, the more custom pieces there are, the harder it would be for a player to identify discrete supporting and opposing actions. We made the experience easier to interpret, but less natural to hear.

We were all happy to finally have this behind us. In comparison to the dialogue system, building a complete, open-ended world of a leadership/meeting situation seemed easy.

Chapter Fourteen

Modeling a Little World

The Physics System

> Even programs with very simple underlying rules
> can yield great complexity.
> —*Stephen Wolfram*, A New Kind of Science

Our universe has rules. The earth revolves, changing the side facing the sun. Magnets can either attract or repel, depending on the alignment.

Local environments and situations require a working knowledge of a more limited set of rules. A good example might be town roads. Cars driving down these roads are subject to a huge number of *physical* forces that operate in parallel:

- Every car has a direction, speed, and center of gravity.
- Cars occupy a certain amount of space; two cars can't occupy the same space at the same time (and I have tried).
- Rain reduces visibility and traction.
- The size of the car impacts acceleration and braking.
- Cars have different turning ability.
- There are fences, houses, and trees that absolutely prevent passage, and grassy yards that merely discourage passage.
- Cars have different top speeds.
- There are straight roads, windy roads, dirt roads—and off-road.

- Gravity keeps cars from jumping too far.
- There are suggested traffic rules, such as speed limits and stopping at a red light.
- There is congestion, severe or light, depending on the number of cars.
- There might be construction.
- There are squirrels.
- Visibility changes from road to road.

As well as the physics, there are drivers who influence these cars. These drivers follow social rules (or not), and *might* be influenced by:

- Getting to a specific destination;
- Being in a hurry;
- Taking an aesthetically pleasing route;
- Caring about safety; and, in some cases,
- Caring about conforming to rules, norms, and laws.

A Large Number of Rules

Simulations describe small worlds. They describe local environments. These worlds have physical properties and usually have some form of inhabitants.

The *physics* systems of simulations comprise a large number of rules to describe the environment. Nothing can be taken for granted with computers, of course, and everything has to be defined.

The number of rules for a simulation ten years ago might have been in the ten's, enough to fill a single page of a spreadsheet. Today's simulations have hundreds or thousands of rules, and the simulations of the future will have tens of thousands of rules. Regardless of the number of rules, the environment will never be fully described, nor should it be.

There is always an editorial decision, not just about the absolute value of the relationships, but also about which rules are captured and which rules are left out. There is also a need to organize the rules, to make later editing and modifications easier.

Modeling "Physics" in a Leadership Situation

Modeling the world for a computer game is hard enough. The challenges we faced in modeling a leadership world were quite different in at least two areas. First, the rules, the *physics*, were social. We could not take a Porsche and a stopwatch and measure the one true value. We had to taperecord and discuss and read and research to come up with approximations.

Second, people, by and large, have spent more time in meetings than they have in most of the contexts portrayed in computer games, such as driving an exotic car down a pristine European road or designing an amusement park. So we had a higher standard to meet in terms of getting "the feel" right. People knew a lot about meetings; they just didn't know that they knew.

At a high level, the factors we most cared about were the relationships between people, power, tension, ideas, and work (Figure 14.1). In the end, we came up with approximately five hundred rules in these five categories.

A Sampling of the Rules for Ideas(see with how many you disagree)

- Ideas are in one of five states: un-introduced, active, paused (if another idea is made active), stopped (if the amount of work is pushed back to 0), passed, or pre-empted.

- Characters introduce ideas, changing their state from un-introduced to active and changing the state of the previously active idea (if there is one) to paused.

Figure 14.1 A High-Level View of the Physics System

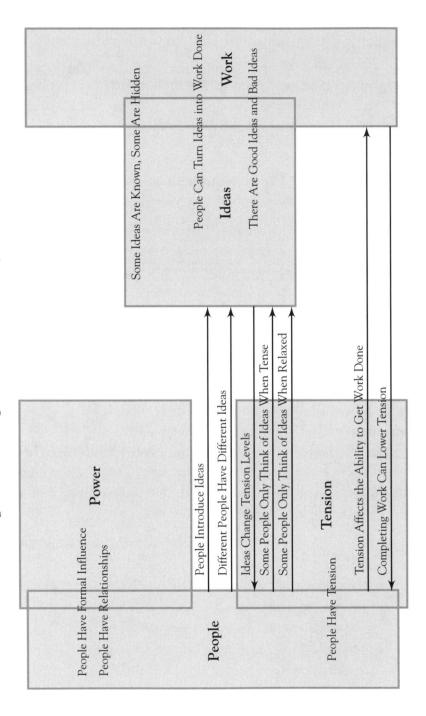

- Some *un-introduced* ideas are only known to certain characters.
- Characters can make a *paused* idea *active* again, changing the state of the previously active idea (if there is one) to *paused.*
- There is at most only one idea active at a given time. If an idea is just passed or just stopped, there can be no active ideas.
- Every character has an opinion about every idea.
- Two or more ideas can be incompatible, which means the *finishing* of one *pre-empts* the others. The *pre-empted* idea can no longer be made *active.*
- Only active ideas can have work done to them.
- One idea is always "Finish Meeting." All characters know this idea.
- People can oppose ideas. If an idea's work level is pushed back to zero, it again becomes a *stopped* idea.
- Some characters only have access to (think of) certain ideas when tense.
- Some characters only have access to (think of) certain ideas when relaxed.

A Sampling of Rules for Work

- Characters can support people and ideas passively as well as actively.
- When the "Finish Meeting" idea is passed, the meeting is over.
- Each idea requires a certain amount of work to be done before the idea is considered complete. That amount is predefined by the idea.
- The amount of work done is increased by the positive work contributed by each character (including mostly active but also passive work), with a bonus for that character's proximity to the Optimal Tension Level and a teamwork bonus for multiple positive contributors. It is lowered by the negative work contributed

by each character, with a bonus for that character's proximity to the Optimal Tension Level.

- People can turn ideas into work done (that is, can pass ideas) by supporting them.
- People can reverse work by opposing an idea.
- Ideas can only be worked on (building or opposing) when they are active.
- Characters have a predefined amount of support/work they can put toward each idea. Some characters cannot pass some ideas by themselves. They need contributions from other characters.
- Once an idea is *passed,* it cannot be made *active* again.
- Once an idea has been *introduced* and then *stopped,* any character can reintroduce it.
- If an idea is *stopped,* it can be re-introduced.

I always do a double take when I read the last item. One of our teammates did not like this rule. I mean she *really* did not like this rule. The first time she called me up went like this:

"We should be able to get ideas permanently off the table, if they are bad enough," she argued. "Ideas do get killed. Great thoughts go away if people don't nurture them."

"I don't want the game to be over in a second if a great idea gets killed," I argued back. "In real life, ideas can be re-introduced." We spent about an hour debating the issue. Finally, she agreed.

Or so I thought.

The next day she sent me some more emails arguing that ideas should be able to be killed permanently. This time, I was more brusque with her. "Executive decision," I wrote back. "Killed ideas can come back." And I moved on.

The next day I found out that she had called some of our programmers and opened up the debate with them. I was furious. "Look," I said, "if ideas could be killed permanently, this idea would have been dead a long time ago!"

My logic prevailed. I finally won. I had unequivocally killed that idea. And proved myself wrong.

A Sampling of Rules for Power
(Although Most Were Handled by the AI)

- Every character has an opinion about every other character.
- Every charter has formal authority.
- Characters can form alliances to strengthen their own power.

A Sampling of Rules for Tension

- Each characters has a tension level.
- Praising someone lowers the person's tension a lot, the tension of their allies a little, and everyone's a bit.
- Criticizing someone raises his or her tension a lot, the tension of allies a little, and that of everyone a bit.
- Tension affects a character's productivity/ability to get work done. Each character is the most productive when he or she is slightly tense, and each player's productivity diminishes as he or she either becomes more relaxed or more tense.
- Completing work lowers everyone's tension.
- The active idea changes the tension levels of all characters. The same idea can have different impacts on different characters. Only active ideas can alter the tension of a room.

A Whole Lot of Simple

It is amazing, when laid out, how simple all of the rules seem. Each one is so basic that it is almost not even worth mentioning. It is only together that they become compelling. To this day, it is a wonder to see how successfully they model the world we sought to simulate.

The other wonderful part about all of the rules is that they are so unpredictable when processed in parallel. The ending results surprise the creators as much as the players.

We had created a wonderful environment. Now we just needed to populate it with corporate executives we could call our own.

Chapter Fifteen

Modeling the Inhabitants

The AI System

> Neuromorphic systems are systems that are
> deliberately constructed to make use of some of
> the organizational principles that are felt to be used
> in the human brain.
> —*James Anderson*, Neurocomputing, *p. xiii*

Humans are pretty well optimized for the planet on which we live. The Earth provides a relatively constant temperature; our acceptable temperature range is pretty narrow and in the middle of what the Earth provides. The light that comes from our star, the sun, is a bit on the yellow side; the cones in our eyes favor that part of the spectrum. The Earth today has oxygen (thanks, plants): we breathe it. Humans make sense, given everything in our environment.

So too must any self-directed inhabitant of a computer-generated environment make sense. Any kind of critter must:

- Have appropriate needs;
- Be attuned to the right stimulation;
- Have appropriate abilities to impact the environment; and ultimately
- Be able to meet his or her needs.

Two Types of Artificial Intelligence

There are two, complimentary types of artificial intelligence in Virtual Leader. One uses a set of fixed rules, very similar to the physics system we developed. The other is a fuzzy logic system closer to the process used by the neurons in our own brain.

The "Fixed Rules" Physics of Virtual Leader's AI

The physics part of the AI system can further be divided into two pieces (sorry). The first, like a sorority, is a dense tapestry of mutual opinions. The second, more like a Zurich political convention, is a commerce system formed around *personal influence*.

A Tapestry of Likes and Dislikes

All of the characters in Virtual Leader have opinions of all of the other characters, and of all of the ideas. They weave together to form a dense tapestry of likes and dislikes.

A character's opinion toward another character increases if:

- They like similar ideas ("Hey, you like antique cars? So do I!").
- They like each other's allies ("Yeah, isn't Chester great?").
- They dislike each other's enemies ("I hate that guy too").
- They dislike the same idea ("Clowns *are* creepy").
- They are liked by authority figures, as influenced by their respect for authority ("The boss likes Ann-Marie; that's good enough for me").

Their opinions of one another decrease if they:

- Dislike similar ideas ("How can you not like monkeys?").
- Dislike each other's allies ("At least he was elected President. What have you done?").

- Like each other's enemies ("How can you like Svetlana? Have you seen her eat?").
- Are not liked by authority figures, as influenced by their respect for authority ("The boss doesn't like Billy-Bob; I am keeping my distance").

Similarly, a character's opinion toward an idea changes in the same way. His or her opinion of an idea increases if it is liked by allies, for example.

The Currency of Personal Influence

The second piece of fixed rules AI system is both simpler and less intuitive (Figure 15.1). As we discussed earlier, there is a currency that all people earn and spend, most of the time without knowing it. It is called *personal influence* (PI).

Characters spend personal influence primarily by changing the focus of the group. Redirecting the focus to a person is pretty inexpensive, from a *PI* perspective, as is bringing up an easy idea. Focusing the group on a controversial idea, in contrast, is quite expensive. In Virtual Leader's AI, as soon as any character spends more than he or she has earned, the bots start increasing their dislike of the character. If a character continues to try to refocus the attention of the group after having burned through all of his or her personal influence, the bots eventually *really* dislike that character.

People earn personal influence by being on the winning side of an argument, by getting an idea accepted, and whenever the group discusses an idea they sponsored. From a personal influence perspective, though, all ideas are not the same. Ideas gather importance as the characters debate them. For example, imagine two high-powered CEOs arguing over where to have the meeting. This issue is relatively unimportant, but the more it is debated without a resolution, the more that rides on the outcome.

Figure 15.1 High-Level View of Fixed Rules in the AI System

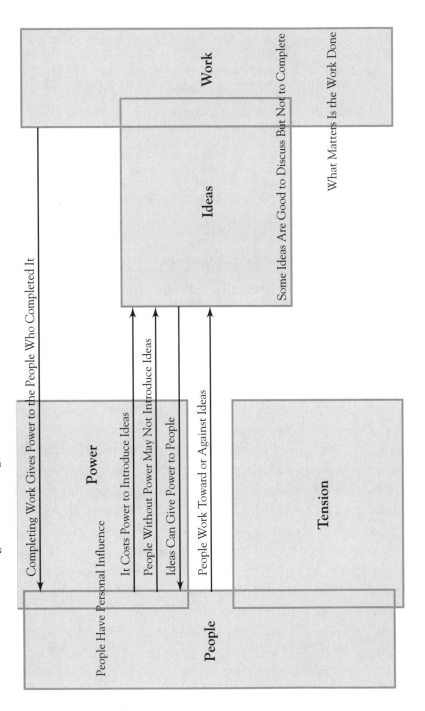

Distributed "All or Nothing" Artificial Intelligence

The second part of the AI system is deeper and creates behavior that is a lot more subtle. At its heart, the bots practice three-to-one leadership. As with Virtual Leader player/learners, the bots care about gaining power, moderating tension, raising ideas, and completing work.

The bots can pursue three-to-one transparently. That means that the players can click on a bot and learn why it is doing what it is doing. That is important, allowing the player to learn from the bots.

To accomplish their goals, the bots use what we call "microstrategies." Each microstrategy increases the chance that a bot will do a given action. For example, if a bot has not met a *power* need, he or she is more likely to:

- Support an idea that the boss likes;
- Introduce an idea;
- Positively support bots that the rest of the group generally like; and/or
- Focus on a playing or paused idea that he or she sponsored.

If not enough ideas have been introduced to meet its *idea* need, the bot is more likely to:

- Introduce an idea and/or
- Try to push the tension in the room to an extreme.

If the tension is above its high *tension* threshold, the bot is more likely to:

- Focus on a calming idea and/or
- Praise people.

If the tension is below its low *tension* threshold, the bot is more likely to:

- Criticize people and/or
- Focus the conversation on tension-filled ideas.

If the bot has met its need for power, ideas, and tension, and not enough good ideas have been passed, the bot is more likely to:

- Try to pass an idea he or she likes.

And most of the time, not connected with any broader need, the bot is more likely to:

- Support an idea or person he or she likes;
- Oppose an idea or person he or she dislikes;
- Not to do anything if tension is too low;
- Not to do anything if tension is too high;
- Not introduce or reintroduce an idea that costs more PI than the bot has; and/or
- Focus on the "end meeting" idea if the meeting has been going on for a while.

At the end of the deliberation, the bot chooses among the highest probability actions. This model assures that all considerations are taken into account, and there is even a bit of randomness.

The microstrategies that contributed to the decision are used to drive the bot's internal monologue, so the player can see why the bot did what it did, all in three-to-one parlance. This method created bots of surprising sophistication and interest.

Distorted Leadership

Designers of computer games complain a lot about pressures of designing the AI of their bots. If they make them too stupid, such as not being aware that the bot next to them was just shot down, the game has no sense of reality. But if the AI is too smart—say, a bot firing at you never misses or it tracks you down perfectly every time you try to escape—the game loses any sense of fun.

We had a similar problem. If the bots were too dumb, they would be unbelievably frustrating to try to lead. If they were too smart, they could maneuver the situation as well as you could, making you unnecessary. We also, consistently enough, wanted to make the AI part of the learning experience interesting as well.

We found the perfect solution: We created distorted three-to-one frameworks for our bots. They all practiced incomplete leadership. Each had high doses of some aspects of three-to-one and not enough of other aspects. This created both interesting and, bizarrely enough, surprisingly accurate models of leadership behavior.

Power Hoarders

We gave some bots an unquenchable thirst for power. Their power microstrategies were always on. They might not be the only microstrategies that were on, but they always influenced every decision.

The high-power bots sucked up to the boss. They talked about their ideas readily and brought the conversation back to their ideas if other people shifted away from them. They cut off people they did not think could help them. They did not care about accomplishing anything.

This is, unfortunately, consistent with real life. And in both Virtual Leader and real life, it also doesn't work. One reason why power hoarding is ineffective is that sharing power is essential for generating ideas. Many junior employees who have great ideas but little political capital, informal authority, or formal authority will not introduce their ideas for fear of having them shot down.

The power grabbers do not realize intuitively that each time they miss a leadership opportunity to help a group complete the right work, their power actually ebbs away. We have all seen people grow increasingly manipulative trying to over-compensate for a lack of results.

Tension Drivers

We similarly defined the ranges of tension each bot would push toward. We made some bots always trying to drive down the tension level. We had other bots always try to drive the tension up.

Again, this leadership behavior has a real-life counterpart. Some people are constantly raising or constantly lowering tension. Some are whirlwinds, making everyone uncomfortable the moment they walk into a room. They make caustic remarks. They focus on the tense issues. Others epitomize calm in their speech and manner and relax everyone around them. They are never angry. They focus the attention on calming ideas. They say nice things.

Sometimes a given tension-raising or tension-lowering strategy can be perfect for a situation. But to apply either type indiscriminately ensures that they miss the mark far too often.

The Great Moderators

We made some bots do a great job at gaining enough power, moderating tension, and generating ideas. But they never actually pulled the trigger on any project. They loved to talk about great things. They loved to go back and forth in dialogues, sometimes heated, sometimes calm.

But they never felt any urge to get anything done. They would rather perpetually analyze than commit. Finally, the only urgency they would feel was to finish the meeting on time and leave the room.

Unfortunately, far too many real-life leaders reflect this penchant—think the stereotypical corporate staffer. People who fit this profile stall the group's progress with their "analysis paralysis" instead of contributing toward taking action.

The Idea People

Some people see their value as coming up with new ideas. They bring up one, then another, then another. They switch between them. They see their ascension in the group and the larger organization as the direct result of coming up with the right idea.

By ratcheting up a bot's need to come up with new ideas and ratcheting down the other needs, we were able to create the perfect example of someone who is flaky and unfocused.

The Producers

Some people view their day as a failure unless they have produced something. Anything. I have talked to more than a few new managers in software divisions of computer companies. I have asked, "How was your day?" They have responded, "Terrible. All I did was talk to people all day. I didn't get anything done."

If we take away a bot's need for power, ideas, and tension, its behavior is very much like the producer. They want to pass three or four ideas (any ideas), and then call an end to the meeting.

Debugging AI

A microstrategies system can be tweaked almost infinitely. Microstrategies can be made more or less powerful and can be influential more or less often. We could also have changed the goals of the various bots to find the right balance against the three-to-one elements.

This was fortunate, because the values that we put in as guesstimates were pretty far off. The microstrategy system took the most fixing of any system in Virtual Leader.

The first iteration of the five meetings looked like a mental ward. Literally. None of the bots talked, they all just periodically looked up at the ceiling. We were also having graphic problems with the Rosa bot. One of her eyes was resting on her chin, giving a disconcerting "Picasso" effect.

In the second iteration, all of the bots talked about their own ideas, with no regard to what anyone else was saying. They would talk at the same time. This looked more like kindergarten.

At one point it became too easy for the bots to engage in mutual obsession. One would praise another, then the second would praise the first. Pretty soon it turned into a love fest, without any work getting done. This felt more like a Hollywood awards dinner.

One time we had other variables mistuned, and bots became too focused on defeating an idea they did not like. We called it the "George Costanza" bug, after Jason Alexander's character in the popular "Seinfeld" sitcom. The bots would introduce ideas just to criticize them. Or a bot would keep returning to an idea he or she did not like, even after the group had moved on to a different topic.

Debugging this kind of AI can drive someone with a big-picture perspective, like me, a little batty. You have to focus on getting a lot of little numbers right. Perhaps my colleagues were telling me something when they decorated my office one day when I was offsite in the theme of the Oscar winning movie A *Beautiful Mind* (Figure 15.2).

Figure 15.2 My Office Decorated with A *Beautiful Mind* Theme

Still, we finally were starting to get it right. One of the most interesting moments came when we were playing with Meeting Three. At one point Oli disagreed with his boss, and his boss's boss, and focused intently on his idea. He was censured from his peers, but he didn't care. He put all of his energy toward this one goal.

It seemed unnatural for a peon to behave this way, so we went into the code. It turned out that he was practicing his version of leadership. He had enough power, he had enough ideas, the tension was perfect for productive work, and now he was willing to do whatever it was going to take to push his priorities through.

On one hand, we admired his spunk. On the other hand, it didn't seem natural, so we had to rip out his moxie. It's not easy being a tiny God.

Part Three

Philosophical and Technical Realities

Chapter Sixteen

A New Look at Work

The Interface System

Time spent inside a simulator is not a picnic.
Simulators are not toys. They are "fun" in some
sense, but only about as much fun as an actual
no-kidding tank.

> —*Bruce Sterling,* War Is Virtual Hell

We had always had some sketches and definite thoughts about how an end-user would engage Virtual Leader. But from a development perspective, the simulation input was one of the last pieces of functionality that we completed.

For all simulations, the interface is a connection between the user and the designer. Through the interface, the designer communicates to the users what tactics they will be performing. The interface represents the parsing of all possible actions into a finite few.

The Objectives of Simulation Input

The area of simulation input is still more art than science. But certain rules and objectives have become increasingly clear.

Objective 1: Represent the Actual Activity at Some Level

The interface to simulations should represent the activity that they are simulating for any cyclic learning to occur. This is an easier task when manipulating physical tools, such as the steering wheel on a car. It requires a bit more creativity when dealing with any kind of soft skills. The reason multiple-choice input doesn't work for simulations is that no one's job consists of deciding among three viable alternatives.

Objective 2: Be Part of the Learning

No matter how well the interface is designed, learning how to use it will require some work from the end-learners before they can even begin to engage the simulation. And it tends to be very high frustration time. To justify the investment of time, the interface, therefore, has to be part of the learning.

Here is a quick test for any design. Could the interface, and perhaps a description of its functionality, stand alone as a textbook diagram? Could the diagram hang on a wall in a classroom? In other words, if the end-learners did nothing but learn the interface for the simulation, they would have learned some useful content. If not, it would be hard to get the end-learners to invest much in the learning process.

Objective 3: Be a "Real" Metaphor

Says SimCity and The Sims creator Will Wright:

> Most of my games use an obvious metaphor and a non-obvious metaphor. People bought SimCity thinking it was like a train set, and the interface reinforced that. That made it accessible. But they come to realize the game was in fact more like gardening. Things sprout up, you had to plant, and you had to weed. Players had to update their mental models to be successful. When you start up The Sims for the first time, it feels like a dollhouse.

In an educational simulation, examples and microcosms may be more important than the metaphors, but all of the thinking remains the same. The meeting place became both a metaphor and a microcosm of a leadership situation.

Objective 4: Keep It Simple and Streamlined

Computer games, especially those aimed at hard-core gamers, can be complicated. They can have combo moves. They can use every key on a keyboard for shortcuts.

For the foreseeable future, educational simulation designers will not have that luxury. The interface has to be simple. Most of the interface should be accessible via the mouse. There should be no scrolling through menus on top of menus. There should be no obscure keyboard commands.

As game legend Warren Spector puts it, "We absolutely must streamline our interfaces and make them so intuitive users forget they're even using an interface. We have to make sure users know exactly what they're supposed to do at all times and challenge them to figure out how."

Visually, the interface is often an interruption of the virtual world. It is something that the player sees and no one else (you can almost imagine a computer character with whom you have been discussing something looking up suddenly at the menu bar and asking, "Hey, has that always been there?"). Even though the goal is invisibility, that is often not possible, so the interface should have a certain well-designed style to it and be consistent with the rest of the experience.

As end-learners become more sophisticated, controls will become more complicated. Until then, simplicity has to be the rule.

Objective 5: Operate in Real Time

End-learners should engage the simulation in real time. Too much learning is lost otherwise. This means that all options are available all the time, which necessarily impacts interface design.

Our Solution: The Opinion Bar

Here's how we brought all of these rules together. The primary interface is what we call an "opinion bar" (Figure 16.1). Every character and every idea in the simulation has an opinion bar (Figure 16.2).

Figure 16.1 The Virtual Leader Opinion Bar

Figure 16.2 All Characters and All Ideas Have Opinion Bars

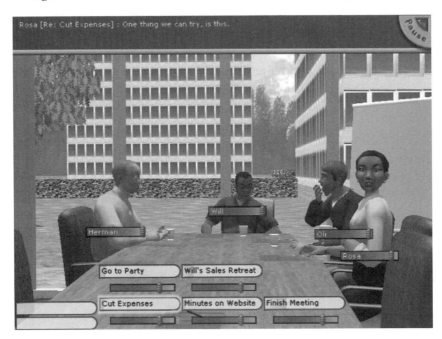

These opinion bars can be clicked at any time during the course of a session. They only require one click to allow the end-learner to fully engage the simulation. Each bar presents a range, from strongly negative in the red area on the left to neutral in the middle to strongly positive in the green right-hand area. Learners can therefore demonstrate subtle gradients if they are so inclined.

At a high and consistent level, the opinion bars serve two functions. They let the users express their opinions, and they let the users focus the attention in the room.

But depending on where and when a player clicks, the functionality—and what the user says—differs significantly. Context is used aggressively and, hopefully, invisibly.

If the player clicks on the green side of an active idea, the player will be *supporting* its progress. If the idea has a lot of support already, the player will *finish* the idea, ending the conversation around it.

If the player clicks on the red side of an active idea opinion bar, the player will be *opposing* its progress. If the idea does not have much support, the player will *stop* the idea, making it harder for anyone else to reintroduce it.

If the player clicks on the green side of a non-introduced or stopped idea, the player will be *introducing* it to the group positively. If the player clicks on the red side of a non-introduced or stopped idea, the player will be *introducing* it to the group negatively.

If the player clicks on the green side of an inactive idea, the player will make that idea active, *reintroducing it positively*. If the player clicks on the red side of an inactive idea, the player will make that idea active, *reintroducing it negatively*.

It is the same process for the people opinion bars (Figure 16.3). If the player clicks on the green side of a person who has recently been talking, for example, he or she will *compliment* what the person has said and ask for more information. If the player clicks on the red side, then he or she is criticizing the person's role in the meeting.

Figure 16.3 Tactics Available Through One Click on Opinion Bar

	Person		Idea	
Focus	Encourage an Active Participant Criticize an Active Participant	Ask for More Information	Work Toward an Active Idea Work Against an Active Idea	Finish an Idea
Switch	Positively Engage a Quiet Group Member Negatively Engage a Quiet Group Member		Switch Topics Positively Switch Topics Negatively	Introduce an Idea

But if the player clicks on the green side of a person who has not recently been talking, he or she will *positively invite the person into the conversation*, ask what the person has said and ask for more information. If the player clicks on the red side, he or she will be criticizing the person's lack of involvement (Figure 16.4).

Figure 16.4 Opinion Bars

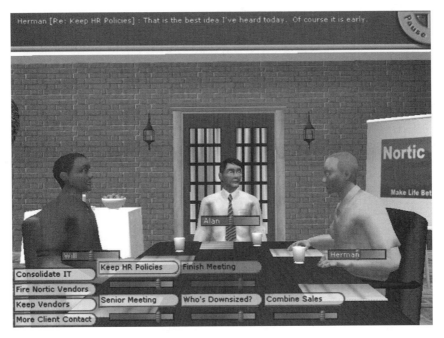

A Model for Work

Very early computer games greatly influenced the design of our modern computer desktop environment. Arcade games introduced a graphical interactivity around dragging and clicking that became a dominant model for all Apple and Windows applications.

In the same way, interfaces around educational simulations will eventually become models of work. Early-adopting sites of Virtual Leader have already begun using phrases like, "You're clicking in my green zone" or "Let's pass that idea." Getting the interface right will not just help people do work, but eventually will impact the very definition of work.

Chapter Seventeen

The Scariest Word of All: Gameplay

> Our original model contained a feedback strategy
> where immediate feedback was provided for even
> the smallest mistake. We learned that while critical
> errors warrant immediate feedback, smaller errors
> can be overlooked or corrected via delayed feedback.
> —*Stephanie Lackey, Interdisciplinary/*
> *Computer Engineer, AIR—4962, NAVAIR, TSD*

What makes a Paris woman a Parisian? Why is the word "monkey" funny? And what makes a computer game engaging?

Gameplay is the ineffable combination of everything that makes some games so engaging. The very word should strike fear in all designers. It encompasses graphics, story, interface, and so much more. More than a few games that seemed to have everything have died unceremoniously because the "gameplay" did not work.

As our work on Virtual Leader progressed, I spent the most time sweating gameplay. The principal design work was done in the summer of 2001. The next six months were spent taking care of programming issues. I would not be able to actually play the program, even an early version of it, until January 2002.

The Waiting Game

While Virtual Leader was crawling toward a playable version, we continued to debate and clarify our thinking on some of the gameplay issues we faced. A basic one was: Can educational content ignore gameplay? After all, the point is to deliver content, not to entertain, some argued. Doing the right thing is doing the right thing. It doesn't have to be exciting, or always a near-miss.

Maybe the stakes in educational simulations weren't quite as high as in the entertainment world, the other side countered. But if everything didn't come together, the program would also soon disappear. Besides, the expectation of any users would be that it would be at least some fun.

Every day I would wonder about it. I had no idea what the feel of the game would be like. How long would a meeting last? Six minutes for a short one, up to twenty minutes for a long meeting seemed right in theory. At this point in our work, though, we had no idea what might happen.

How intense would Virtual Leader be? Could you play it with one hand as you were filling out an expense report, or would you have to be quite focused?

There were so many questions from a gameplay perspective. What parts would be satisfying? What parts would be hard? What parts would be easy? What feedback would be clear? What kinds of hints would we have to give?

How would each level of meeting play out? The situations were set, the quotes were written and recorded, but how would they all fit together?

What would be obvious or subtle? What would seem complicated? Had we forgotten some major something? Dialogue? Movements? Relationships?

Once I finally had a copy to play with, I dug in full-force.

Core Ideas

The easiest part of the design was simply designating some ideas as "must passes." These are the ideas that, if you do not pass, you will achieve a very low business results score. From a gameplay perspective, the idea has to be hard to actually uncover, hard to pass, or hard to recognize as a key idea (Figure 17.1).

Figure 17.1 Not Many Ideas Known

Triggers

I went into the simulation design loving the complicated shifting of relationships. To me, the shifting of alliances and opinions seemed to be realistic and open-ended. I still like that level of gameplay.

But I have a new love of triggered events. Triggered events, akin to Easter Eggs, are the predictable, sudden introduction of linear elements that both move the story ahead and open up new aspects of the experience. They are easy to plan and debug, and they convey unequivocal progress to the end-user. The most dramatic triggered event that we used was the appearance of a new idea.

Listen to Everybody

One way for a level designer to "hide" an idea for a dramatic triggered appearance is to give a great idea to a certain bot, especially one that no one likes, who has no PI. Then the bot's expressiveness can be lowered, making him or her less likely to talk. Finally, the designer could either give all of the remaining bots little interest in generating ideas at all or could specifically cripple the microstrategy of engaging the unengaged.

Now the player needs to recognize the quiet bot, bring him or her into a conversation so that the bot would have enough PI to introduce an idea.

Push Tension to an Extreme

Another way we hid ideas for learner/players to find was to associate them with tension. Learner/players would have to significantly calm people in a nerve-wracking environment or raise the tension in a comatose room to get a participant to introduce a great idea (Figure 17.2).

Figure 17.2 A Low-Tension Environment

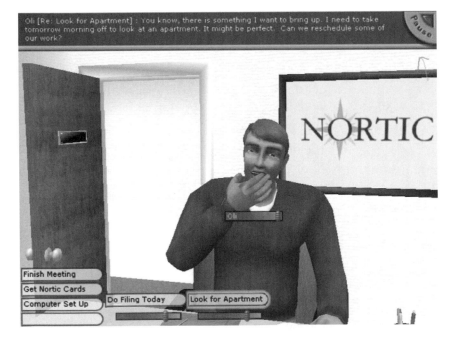

Relationships Are Harder

Our work on the gameplay aspects of core ideas and trigger events was not all that difficult but very satisfying. Helping the player work the tapestry of opinions was much harder, because it was incremental.

The Unifying Idea

There are times to bring a group together. This could be an idea that everybody likes at least a little. As long as someone, such as the player, focuses on this idea, everyone will be brought together because everyone is engaged, at least to some degree (Figure 17.3).

Figure 17.3 Everyone Is Engaged

The Divisive Idea

There were some times when a faction needs to be split. There might be one person who absolutely hates an idea that you need to pass. That person can drag down the entire group, unless you first focus on the idea wedging the group.

When It Is Better to Linger than Rush

One interesting effect in Virtual Leader was that, as with life, it did not always pay to go through an idea as quickly as possible. Sometimes lingering on a calming idea was better than ripping through it, for example.

Tactics and Strategies

Most important of all our gameplay considerations, the simulation was able to accurately replicate the subtleties of leadership situations. Every tactic, everything that the player did, had multiple effects. Some the player probably might want to accomplish and some he or she might not.

For example, praising a person (one click in the green zone) could:

- Calm him or her;
- Calm the room;
- Increase the player's alliance with that person;
- Decrease the player's alliance with that person's enemies; and even
- Transfer a bit of personal influence from the player to him or her.

Finishing off an idea might:

- Give the player some personal influence;
- Calm the room a bit;

- Get rid of a popular idea that was distracting everyone; but it might also

- Take the only idea that increased people's tension off the table, risking having the group drift into a nonproductive love fest.

The Gnaw of a New Genre

In fine-tuning the gameplay of Virtual Leader, I gained a lot of sympathy for all the people involved in creating new genres in the computer game world. The pang of the unknown could be gnawing.

As I learned, there are three almost inevitable events that will occur. All are frustrating.

The first is that, as you finalize gameplay, you will morph the experience from the original idea. Therefore, in the design process, you will have inevitably spent too much energy on one part of the experience and not enough on another.

The second is that you will undoubtedly have missed some critical tool or feature for improving or refining the learner/player experience. This tool might have been easy to add into the equation at the beginning of the project, but is now too expensive and time-consuming to build in after the fact.

The third is that end-users almost always find something that is missing that you never even considered, yet it would improve the experience immeasurably. The obviousness to everybody else makes your missing it even more embarrassing.

Such is the challenge of forging into new genres. There is a nice corollary to this third rule, however. And that is that new people will also be able to look at the simulation and the whole genre through new eyes and exploit it in ways that you never dreamed about. That might be the most satisfying part of all.

Chapter Eighteen

Why Use Grades, Anyway?

Metrics, Scores, and Simulations

I took all of the gut courses I could find and made a
mighty effort to pass. In the end, however, I owed
my graduation to Dean Arnold. He must have
decided, "This guy is improving a bit. Best give him
a diploma and wish him well."

> —*Thomas J. Watson, Jr.*, Father, Son & Co:
> My Life at IBM and Beyond

Almost all formal learning programs have grades. And we were creating a formal learning program. So we needed grading, right?

On the other hand, we were using computer games to teach, and we made up our own leadership theory, so what did we care about convention? Could we push our luck a bit further?

Cultural assumptions aside, was scoring inherent in learning? Did it help or hurt the process? My own feeling about scores and grades is deeply ambivalent, and I put off confronting this issue from a design perspective for as long as possible.

The Grade Debates

Today's computer entertainment has evolved directly from the machines found in local bowling alleys or convenience stores. Scores were critical.

Players received points for killing, for surviving, for miles passed or tiles played, for levels cleared and bonus objectives met. Scores served a multitude of important roles.

Scores triggered extra players and extended play. This provided a nice incentive, and also provided a way for very advanced players to play some games forever.

Scores provided a direct link between the player and the game designer with regard to the value system. Whatever was rewarded was considered a *good* thing, while what was not rewarded was *not* so important.

Perhaps most ostensibly, scores provided bragging rights and set the bar. Early pinball machines maintained the highest score in memory, and flashed it between players. This was a challenge for all others to beat. On the cabinet of some pinball machines and early arcade games, proud players would carve their scores and initials into the sides of the walls or game cabinets. Finally, the designers of Asteroids (released in 1979) built in that functionality. Now the games themselves displayed the top ten scores, with the initials of the people who achieved them.

Arcade games influenced home computer games immeasurably. The first hook of personal systems was to play these games at home. Powerhouse Electronic Arts originally made games for Commodore's Amiga computers. An early advertisement promised that you would be able to "play Marble Madness™ in your bathrobe."

Soon, however, game designers began to build experiences optimized around the new home environment. Clearly, winning free games was not an incentive. Past the sunk cost of hardware and software, all of the games were free. Going deeper and deeper into a game was initially an incentive, but pretty soon people who bought games realized that they had the right to play the entire experience, not just as far as their skills dictated.

And Then Came Doom

The game Doom was revolutionary in more ways than anyone could count. It was the first real First Person Shooter. It embraced cheating (just type in some code for more power, to skip a level, to become invincible). It looked 3D (game-level designer purists argue that height was just an illusion, but it worked for me). It used a free "demo" to entice people to buy the game that was an extensive and brilliant game by itself.

And it also put quite a few nails in the coffin of onscreen scoring. The goal now was to make it to the next level, not to rack up points. The use of scoring has withered away to a point at which it is considered a retro-feature on those few new programs that use it.

Summer Camp and the Purpose of Grades

I worked for four summers at The Chewonki Foundation. For twenty-five years (including when I was there), it was run by Tim Ellis, who turned Chewonki from a little summer camp, in the words of *Down East* magazine, into "a center of progressive environmental education, a learning institute praised as one of the best of its kind in the country."

The staff was filled with both teachers and non-teachers. Every year, we debated about grades. *What was their purpose?* Were they to motivate? Were they a disciplinarian crutch? If so, what did that say about our content and processes?

Why were students graded and instructors were not, especially since the students' parents were paying for their experience? What happened if a student received great grades in every class but one? What did that say about those instructors? Did grades reflect the student or the instructor?

Was the purpose of grades to rank students? If so, what was the value add of an instructor, as opposed to an evaluator? Could the same person morally hold both roles? Should an instructor both elevate and evaluate the level of elevation? In that case, who watches the watchman?

Should grades be diagnostic? If so, giving one grade as opposed to a suite made no sense.

Should there instead be a pass/fail method, with the goal to bring everyone up to a certain competency? If so, what about the boys who came in already above that level?

Should grades mark absolute levels of achievement? Or improvement? Or attitude? Or work ethic? Or willingness to clean up after everybody else after everybody else left?

What is the impact of the outside environment? Should a student who takes one class and has no other obligations receive the same grade for the same work as a student who has five classes and an outside job?

How do you grade when people work as a team? Does everybody receive the same grade? That is never fair. Or do you just discourage teamwork to avoid having to deal with the problem?

What is the need for consistency of grades across instructors? What is the process to ensure the consistency? Is an "A" in one class the same as an "A" in another?

Is it acceptable to a teacher to give all "A's" to his or her class? Is it acceptable to give all "C's" and "D's?" Or should an instructor always use the bell curve for distribution?

Should a student try to optimize grades? Or learn the most? We all knew in college pre-meds or candidates for high academic scholarships who took only classes in which they were assured of receiving a top mark.

We never reached a satisfactory answer to these questions. And up in Wiscasset, Maine, to this day, ten years after I left, the debate continues. As it does—or should—among those who call themselves educators, from elementary school classrooms to the virtual world of high-level soft-skill development.

How Do You Score an Open-Ended Simulation?

I have to admit (and please don't tell anyone) that one reason for my reluctance to incorporate scoring into Virtual Leader was that I really did not know how to do it. How would you score The Sims if you had to? If an experience is open-ended, how do you take into account that one player focuses on wealth and another on social networks? Do you make an equation to say that every $10 thousand in annual income equals two close friends?

How would you score SimCity? Fiscal restrain or expansionary vision? Or the establishment of cultural landmarks?

Should the score be running all of the time, or only at the end? If it is ongoing, how would you measure someone who is executing a more complicated plan than the norm? In open-ended simulations, all of the pieces have to be in place before any results are seen. If scoring is held until the end, who would care? The game is over. Sid Meier's Alpha Centauri gives players a comprehensive score at the end, but at that point, it just doesn't matter.

There is the philosophical question of *what* to reward. But there is also a very technical question of what values you assign. As you add complexity, gameplay becomes harder to predict. Scores seem impossible to create in a way that does not seem arbitrary. How do you take into account all variables? The more complicated and intertwined a system is, by the way, the harder it is.

Here is a real example. In Roller Coaster Tycoon, players have the goal of building their own amusement park, with one core metric being the satisfaction of all of the people at your park. Different people have different needs, and therefore your park may sit better with people who want slow rides, balloons, and leisurely walks by the pond, as opposed to those who crave fast rides and sugary foods. So measuring and scoring customer satisfaction sounds simple enough. But here is a real hint from a site called gamewinners.com on how to increase your park rating: "Find all of the guests who are unhappy or angry. Drown them. Eventually your park rating will go up 100 to 200 points."

Tight metrics and open-ended play seemed like impossible bedfellows. As Virtual Leader evolved, I also continued to have the fear that someone would sit down, pound randomly on the keyboard for ten minutes, and end up with a great score.

It wasn't getting any easier.

The Continuing Adventure

While I was always uncomfortable with scoring, I also always intended for players to find out what happened next as a result of their actions. If people were to make choices, we wanted the experience to give them feedback with regard to those choices, which we dubbed a "story line continuation" (Figure 18.1).

Figure 18.1 A Poor Virtual Leader Story Line Continuation

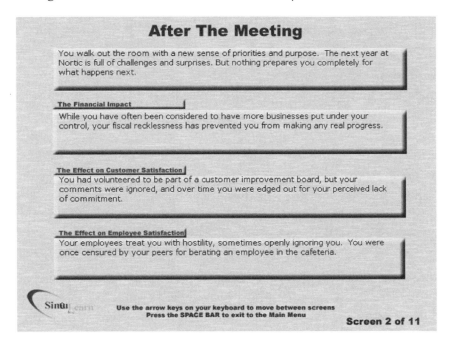

My hope was that through this story line continuation, I would not have to deal with numerical metrics. Based on feedback from many sources, I soon realized this was a battle I was going to lose. We needed to come up with a more robust system.

Cause (Leadership) and Effect (Business Results)

We split up our evaluation of what met performance standards into two categories. The first was leadership, which sought to measure how well a player did with power, tension, and ideas. The second was business results, which dealt exclusively with the nature of the ideas that were passed.

For leadership, we looked at a graph of a player's performance throughout the meeting. At any given point, we looked at how many ideas that person had uncovered, how close to a productive tension he or she had come, the group's opinion of him or her, and personal influence. We called the sum of these numbers, a player's *leadership potential*.

We then looked across the entire meeting and found the point where this line was the highest. This was a player's moment of highest leadership potential. We used the scores of a player's power, tension, and ideas at that point to be reflected in the leadership score (Figure 18.2).

Figure 18.2 Change in Leadership Potential

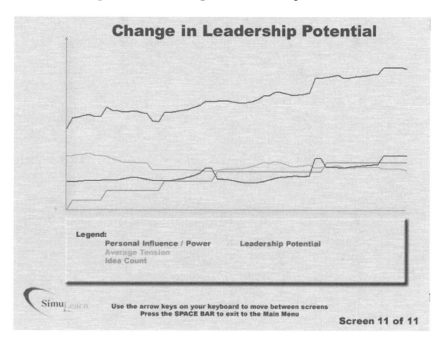

In a really bad situation, a person's highest point of leadership potential was when he or she walked into the room. Some people just went downhill from there.

The best scores, however, were not a gradual, incremental increase. The graph might flatten or dip as a person argued some big point, and the chart would spike up if he or she won that debate.

Most telling, the best players had a leadership potential score that actually dipped significantly at the end of the meeting. This is because, as with life, they were spending that leadership potential toward achieving business results, not hoarding and accumulating the potential for its own sake. Although leadership potential in a given situation can be measured by effective use of power, tension, and ideas, for it to grow in the long term, business results have to follow.

We put mathematical weights into this *leadership potential* graph to treat all three subcategories the same and then averaged them to find a final Leadership Score, but those weights are easy to change to reflect any organization's relative value on those issues.

The *business results* piece of the equation was much simpler. We identified three generic business priorities: customer satisfaction, financial performance, and employee satisfaction. These could compete for resources in the short term but were all necessary in the long term. These could also very easily be customized to meet the specific strategic or balanced scorecard priorities of any organization.

Then, for each idea, we assigned three values. If a given idea were passed, its values were put in the respective customer satisfaction, financial performance, and employee satisfaction scores. These three categories were averaged for a single Business Results score. Finally, the Leadership and Business Results scores were averaged for a final score.

We also had to add a new rule to our physics system:

- *Physics Rule:* Ideas passed impact your Business Results score in three categories: customer satisfaction, employee satisfaction, and financial performance.

Normalizing Around Grades

As with everything, though, even the straightforward factors arouse interesting debates. Take a look at a piece of one player's score breakdown at the end of a Virtual Leader session, shown in Table 18.1.

Table 18.1 Part of a Player's Score from Virtual Leader

Business Results		
Financial Performance	90%	
Customer Satisfaction	95%	
Employee Satisfaction	80%	
Results Total		90%

There are at least two assumptions that most people make. The first is that the scores for *financial performance*, *customer satisfaction*, and *employee satisfaction* fall into a standard A, B, C, D, or F grading range. That is, 60 to 69 is considered a barely passing D, where 70 to 79 is an "average" score of C (although not at Harvard), 80 to 89 is a good B, and 90 to 100 is the top range.

There is nothing inherently natural about this schema, especially with regard to simulation development. In an open-ended environment, a score can be 120. Or 30. Or even a negative 100. We had to add a significant amount of translating logic to push and restrain the scores to a range that most people consider natural. This always involved more editorializing then anyone wanted.

The second assumption that people will make is that the three numbers for *financial performance*, *customer satisfaction*, and *employee satisfaction* will average out to the Business Results total.

Either or both assumptions can be challenged, but to do so takes work on the part of the end-learner. And even with explanation, the more the simulation deviates from familiar norms, the more a learner tends to regard the results as suspect. In other words, *more accurate scoring that breaks the expected norms of the end-learner will be treated as less accurate.* And, of course, if players were doing the translating in their own heads back to their own version of good and bad scores, why shouldn't we do it for them?

Having said that, here is a specific dilemma that we faced. All of the ideas passed either contributed toward or against the three components of a player's Results scores—financial performance, customer satisfaction, and employee satisfaction.

We did have the luxury of hard-coding values with ideas. In other words, the ideas that passed all contributed a set number (Table 18.2).

Table 18.2 Sample Scores for Business Results Components

	Financial Performance	Employee Satisfaction	Customer Satisfaction
Keep focus on Call Center	20	20	30
Rosa on Sales Call	5	15	10
Rosa put minutes on Website	5	–10	–5
Go to Party together	0	5	0
Cut short term expenses and increase reserve	10	–10	–5
Focus on Will's Sales Retreat	–10	10	5
Finish Meeting	60	60	60

I thought one great aspect of a simulation would be to have players choose subtly among the three business subcategories of employee satisfaction, customer satisfaction, and financial performance. The problem was that if we capped each of the three scores at 100 and we wanted to use an averaging equation, then the best high score we could get was around 88 percent. So we had to make a high of 105 possible.

When to Score

A very large issue was when to score. We wanted players to try new behaviors, not just to play conservatively.

We looked at several models:

- *Track first and last:* We could track a person's first score and last score. This had the advantage of showing improvement, which we could use as some sort of internal marketing.
- *Track every score/take the best:* We could encourage people to play often. This seemed too "easy," however, and opened up the possibility of people playing it randomly and hitting upon a successful meeting once that they could never repeat again.
- *Track every score/take the average:* We could keep track of all the scores and then average them. This would encourage people to keep playing and practicing. But it would still put people in a conservative mindset.

The other issue was, given the series of five meetings, how would we play them out? When would a player move on? Did a player need to have a certain score to unlock the next meeting? Or would it happen automatically?

We finally decided on a system that was simple and effective. Here are our rules:

- You can practice by playing a meeting as often as you would like. You see your full metrics, but these scores are not tracked.
- When you feel ready, you commit to playing a scoring round. This score is tracked.
- Once you play a scoring round, the next meeting is unlocked.
- After you have played a scoring round for a given meeting, you can never play a scoring round for that meeting again.

Tracking Everything

I had always thought being able to detect biases for customer satisfaction, financial performance, or employee satisfaction as short-term goals would be useful to an enterprise, in knowing which way someone naturally leaned. Perhaps the wrong person ended up in receivables, and he or she should be out in front of prospects instead.

The nice thing about a real-time environment is that events happen so quickly that people tend to make intuitive rather than intellectual choices. The guards that most of us have built up are brought down. The more subtle the interface, the more people don't realize that they are even making a choice. They think that they are walking a straight line, along the same path as everyone else, when in fact they are veering off dramatically.

By making relatively small changes to the Virtual Leader code, an employer could track a startlingly large number of facts about a user. For example, the employer could track:

- General positive or negative tendencies;
- Positive or negative actions toward other people, sorted by race, gender, or even attractiveness; and
- Active versus passive management style.

As we become more savvy with regard to simulations, more people will probably spend more time being suspicious. At least for now, people are wonderfully naïve. That's not a bad thing—it means that people tend to be open-minded enough to use exciting technology like Virtual Leader to develop all sorts of skills vital to successful leadership in today's organizations.

Chapter Nineteen

Virtual Leader vs. the World

Nineteenth-century mathematicians discovered to their discomfort that as the conceptual machinery of mathematics became more precise, it became more difficult.
   —*David Berlinski*, The Advent of the Algorithm

After almost two years of work, my partners and the SimuLearn salespeople began taking Virtual Leader to prospective customers in the summer of 2002. It was a singularly miserable process.

I knew that when I undertook the development of our leadership simulation that not only would I learn about simulations, but I would also learn about the hidden assumptions of e-learning. What I also ended up learning about was all hidden assumptions held by e-learning evaluators.

Taking the Show on the Road

Most people to whom we showed this (many of them friends of mine) had been around e-learning for a while. They were pretty comfortable with their knowledge of the field. They thought they had seen it all. They believed they knew what e-learning could and could not do. So we would set up an hour-long appointment, but many really thought they could understand any piece of content in about two minutes.

During the first minute they wanted to know about the brands. "So whose theory are you using?" they would ask.

"It's a best-of-breed approach."

"Oh," they would say. I could see that we had failed the first question. I could see them making a big red "x" on their mental evaluation form.

Then, in the second minute, they wanted to know what the look and feel was. They wanted to know whether it was text, PowerPoint, Flash, or video. Was it linear sequencing or was it branching?

I'd show them a minute of gameplay. Virtual Leader is visually dense. There is a lot going on simultaneously. And like a computer game or military simulation, or even like a person hitting the tennis ball against the backboard, engaging it was key. Watching it was too removed. People were confused.

"Do you want to try it?

"Oh, no," they would say.

"Go on," we would coax.

"I don't think so," they would say, rolling back in their chairs and even moving their hands away from the mouse, in case we made a mad push to try to get them to play. "It's interesting," they would nod.

And that would be the end of it.

I can't say that I really blamed them. We were doing a terrible job at presenting Virtual Leader. We wasted even more time trying to create the proverbial elevator speech—the pithy thirty-second reason why a CEO-level person would want this now. The bad news was that we never came up with it. The good news was that we were never trapped in an elevator with a CEO, so maybe it did not matter.

Virtual Leader was just so new, and we were all so close to it. We represented a new theory of leadership, a new model of work, a new way of learning all at once. And so many of the words ("learn by doing," "simulation," "active learning," "e-learning that works," "engaging") had been used before by vendors.

And I was not unsympathetic. Two years earlier, I was the same way as an evaluator. Most people, whether part of an in-house training function or from a third party supplier, have a job like mine was at Gartner. They have to get to the truth of what a vendor is offering. We have all been burned multiple times in the past for supporting new ideas too enthusiastically.

Missing the Good Old Days

Hitting Virtual Leader's open-ended play right off the bat frustrated a lot of people. Despite the fact that the game mirrored life, faced with the ability to do almost anything, some people recoiled. Open-ended was just so, well, open-ended. Some of them clearly wished for the good old days of multiple choices.

Others wanted to directly, rather than indirectly, control the situation. "Where's the button to give you more power?" several people asked. Or, "What do I press to get more ideas in the discussion?"

Bill Dyas, a simulation consultant to the Navy, gave us some great advice on this issue: "Simulations need to be in different modes. There should be lock-step methods for apprentices and modes that allow completely free play for the masters."

We would eventually build an automated, annotated walkthrough of some successful meetings. This allowed new players to see what they were supposed to press on and what they were supposed to pay attention to in a pressure-free environment. We also created so-called "batting cages," where people could practice specific maneuvers as often as they wanted.

People Will Micromanage

When we were sometimes successful in getting people to play, watching the different play styles was always fascinating.

Some people micromanaged. They burned through their personal influence quickly, accomplishing a key task and building resentment from the crowd they were trying to lead, as they always controlled the conversation.

There Is the Staffer Mentality

Some people used a technique that we since dubbed "the staffer mentality." They showed a behavior that I saw far too often in real corporate life.

These people hated actually committing to, or passing, an idea. Instead they became uncomfortable as progress was being made.

"I want more information," they would say. Or, "Can I research this more?" "How can I learn more about this?" They would volunteer suggestions for the experience. "You should be able to switch modes to go into a library to find out more about the idea" or "I can't go forward without knowing more."

They were right. Research is critical to decision making. And yet, there are moments of truth where you just have to commit. You can learn more, but you ultimately have to decide. Management, as with leadership, is about making decisions with imperfect information. They didn't like that part. Some wanted to analyze forever.

Some Successes

There were a lot of wonderful moments as well. Tom and I were showing the simulation to an Ivy League business school professor. She understood the concepts immediately and wanted to play. We put her into Meeting One, where she took on the role of a new manager giving orders to Oli, the annoying legacy employee. As is typical of some first-time players, she over-controlled the situation, accomplished her tasks, but didn't listen much and didn't share responsibility. In her post-meeting debriefing, she was told that Oli had been irked and had bad-mouthed her to his colleagues after he left the room (Figure 19.1). What was worse, her score was below average.

The professor was a little irked herself. "How dare Oli say those things?" she demanded, pacing across the room. "I am his boss. I did nothing wrong." Then she stopped. "I gave him orders, and he is to obey."

Figure 19.1 An Irked Oli

"Although . . ." she hesitated as she recalled, "there was a situation like this the other day. There was a grad student who was on my research team. He didn't do any work, so I took his name off the final paper." She paused, clearly remembering the situation.

"He was furious. He came in the door," she said, pointing, "and had the nerve to demand to have his name put on. I explained to him as clearly as I could why that was not going to happen. He left when he realized he wasn't going to get his way."

She paused again: "And you know, I bet he spent the next two hours complaining about me as well." She looked back at the computer screen. "I would not have gotten a very good score on that meeting, either."

As we gained more and more insight from demonstrating Virtual Leader on the road, the question became: How could we convince people that it was not what they thought? How could we get people to learn from the simulation, instead of evaluating it against an old model? How could we help more of our prospects to have experiences like the professor's?

Symposia

Jane Boston, general manager, Lucas Learning Ltd., is credited with saying:

> The most critical elements of a simulation come after the game itself. Debriefing what has happened—what a player experienced, felt during the simulation, and is feeling afterwards, what strategies were tried and what happened, what other strategies might have been applied, what else the player needed to know or be able to do, analogies to real-life situations, how the players' own values and experience influenced their actions—are all important items for discussion.

I spent weeks learning how right Jane Boston was. It doesn't take one minute to evaluate Virtual Leader. Or one hour. It probably takes about seven hours. You can only understand it by engaging it yourself. That is what SimuLearn Vice President Graham Courtney realized when he pushed a solution to our problem.

"Virtual Leader wasn't for the weak hearted," Graham said, recounting some early resistance, "and people who were evaluating it almost instinctively kept their distance because they knew the power of what was in front of them. They didn't want to see themselves—and least of all have their colleagues see them—fail in Virtual Leader."

So instead, he wanted to offer a day-long, stand-alone, open-to-the-public leadership symposium. He built an agenda, brought in friends, and tested it again and again. The first few hours were spent discussing the model. The rest of the time was spent, hands-on, with the simulation.

I hated the idea. It was directly contrary to the entire notion of e-learning. It also trapped us in service mode. I fought the idea fiercely. And I was dead wrong.

Before Graham's brainchild, when we had given a Virtual Leader demonstration disk to a training or HR manager after a sales call, our success rate was insignificantly small. Most would not install it, or they would try it once and get distracted.

After a symposium, however, people were hooked. They were inspired in the morning and put some experience under their belt; all afternoon, they would hit some challenging situations, and then resolve them.

The symposium format also gave us a chance to see our prospects' transformation first-hand. Watching the "aha's" was a rewarding part of the process. Listen to a couple of Graham's examples:

- A fifty-year-old architect, a senior member of an established firm, pointed out that in architecture, when you propose how a skyscraper is going to look, its very difficult to get your idea heard unless you are the most powerful person in the group (Figure 19.2). After working with Virtual Leader, he realized that by applying the principles involved, his team had a better idea of how to get their ideas heard. Incidentally, as much as he loved the program, he chose not to share the experience with anyone but his immediate colleagues, because of the advantage he believed it gave him.

Figure 19.2 Learning About Power

- Another situation involved two people who came to the symposium together. We partnered them on one machine. The more aggressive insisted on engaging the simulation first. She didn't take much advice from anyone around her, and did badly. She tried to control everything. After an hour, she was interrupted by a cell phone call and stepped away. Her partner, who had been watching the mistakes her colleague was making, took over. She moved though the first meeting successfully, getting a 90 percent score in the first pass.

- A senior vice president took what he had learned to directly allow him to address an old and tiring business relationship. He was able to understand clearly that it wasn't the person he disagreed with, but the ideas being presented.

Not all the participants in our symposia had a smooth time of it. A consultant who showed up late to the workshop expected to be able to sail through the meetings successfully. His failure became very public by his own volition, and several other people in the group understood him a lot better after an hour on Virtual Leader than they had from working with him in a work group for months.

"The funny thing to me," Graham said to sum it all up, "was that when I embarked on the workshops I thought that people would want to spend more time on the traditional content. But the resounding comment was, 'Please, please spend more time in the simulation.' So now two-thirds of the workshops are driven by the sim, and we are looking to take some of the traditional material out of the workshop so that it's closer to the whole day. My primary role as a facilitator is to mentor in one-on-one situations and to make sure that people make it through any pain involved in behavioral change."

Soon Graham was rolling it out internationally. The seminars more than paid for themselves, and they accomplished two critical goals:

1. They built up a growing group of people who were passionate about the simulation.

2. They showed corporate training types how to roll it out within their own organizations.

The symposia turned out to be absolutely critical to the success of Virtual Leader. As dozens of organizations have rolled out Virtual Leader as an integral part of their leadership development programs, the seminar has provided a critical and flexible template.

In my defense, though, I still think I was a little right. I believe the next generation of students will know from experience how to learn from simulations, the same way they know how to take notes in a classroom. But until then, we have to do a lot of hand-holding.

Part Four

The Way Ahead

Chapter Twenty

Seventeen Simulation Issues

A game with high production values can range
in cost from several hundred thousand dollars
to over $4 million in development costs alone.
Development time also has a broad range.
Depending on size and complexity and art load,
a complex game can take years to complete. I
usually think of a range between twelve and
twenty-four months as typical.

—Jane Boston

Development budgets vary widely from studio
to studio, publisher to publisher, and country to
country. In the United States, for a triple-A title,
you're talking anywhere from a couple million
dollars to over ten million. In Europe, I think
budgets tend to be somewhat lower, and in Asia,
they are lower still.

—Warren Spector

Ten million is closer. Online stuff is even worse.
To make the game 10 percent more polished costs
twice as much. And the only people to notice that
extra polish are hard core gamers. It is like one of
those NASA things—the space shuttle was three
times the complexity of Apollo, but ten times
harder to build.

—Will Wright

Why Aren't There More Simulations Then?

Simulations are powerful tools that will change education. But there are many issues that will dog simulation developers and learner/players for quite some time.

1. Free Play Versus Guided Play

One of the biggest long-term issues will be, How much do you help your users along? How much do you mentor them? How rich should the instructions be? If you guide them too much, the point of the simulation falls away. Now they are getting linear instruction again, and just mindlessly carrying out orders. If you guide them too little, they could get lost, be unclear of what happened or what their goals are. They also might miss out on critical parts of learning.

2. Dynamic Versus Linear Skills

Most classrooms and books teach linear, or process, skills. Simulations teach dynamic skills.

Most managers would fully acknowledge that *their* jobs are made up of dynamic skills. They have to make a hundred judgment calls a day, balancing a long list of interwoven variables. Process skills did not do them any good, they admit, because their days were never the same twice.

These same managers, however, view *their employees*, even long-term, seasoned employees, as needing just linear, process skills. (Of course, if you asked the employees, they would tell you their jobs were also dynamic, with no two days for them, either, ever being the same.)

The "what is good for me is not good for you" mentality is everywhere. Some managers even think that although they "get" simulations, they would be too hard for their workers.

This paternalism is familiar. I did my undergraduate study at Brown University in Providence, Rhode Island. My adoptive father was a trustee at Brown, which no doubt helped me get in. It also gave me another insight into schools. I would on occasion go with him to trustee events, and a pattern became clear. The administration of Brown worked very hard to keep separate the trustees and the students.

There were different buildings for the two groups. Many meetings were off-campus. Most telling, the university scheduled many meetings at "low student activity" times, such as 8:30 on a Sunday morning.

That is one reason why football games were so popular. The trustees gathered away from the students' section, watching the students play from a great distance, so they could talk about the institution. The administration loved this tightly managed situation.

The cobra/mongoose relationship between trustees and students is understandable. The trustees, like all managers, wanted the programs more rigorous, linear, predictable, process-centric, and traditional (although they would never actually sit in a classroom themselves). The students, like employees, wanted courses that were more relevant and open-ended.

I designed Virtual Leader to be the open-ended experience that I craved as an underclassman. Having seen the reaction to it, I admit we had to add a bit of trustee-inspired regimen!

3. Identifying Appropriate
Subject-Matter Experts and Designers

If today's subject-matter experts and e-learning designers are not up to snuff, where do we find the next generation? Simulations require a new way of thinking about content that may never truly be understood from the last generation.

4. Sabbatical, Not Seamless

Training departments have been pressured over the years to reduce the length of their programs. Classes that used to take two weeks were cut to one. One-week classes were reduced to two and a half days. Most programs are now down to two hours. e-Learning has accelerated this pressure. Through customization and smaller pieces of content, we expect a piece of content, a single moment of understanding, to be delivered when and where we want it, preferably while we are still writing the email to a client. Ten minutes is acceptable, but five minutes, or thirty seconds, is better. Some people say the analogy for this model is the movie *The Matrix*. I worry that it is more like the drive-through at McDonald's.

Simulations represent a "back to the future." They are never the fastest way to learn something, because they allow mistakes. Worse, they demand our attention. They require that we take mini "learning sabbaticals," as briefly as twenty minutes or as much as four or five hours. They may even require (parents, cover the ears of your children) a phone-free environment.

5. Simulations Are Hard

A hidden assumption of traditional e-learning is that it is meant to be easy. There should be no furrowing of the brow (except around technical and access issues). According to traditional e-learning dogma, pages should be turned with little friction.

This is more of a holdover from the classroom model than we might like to admit. Take a look at people walking into a classroom. They act like passengers boarding an airplane. They have revved down their own intellect. They are in passive mode.

Simulations will be challenging. They cause frustration. They will cause some mulling. They should be exhilarating.

Approaching a simulation is more like being late for a meeting and having a car that won't start. Passivity isn't an option. The minds of the participants should be in overdrive, peppered with fear and drive, with the most successful thinking, "Bring it on!"

6. Supported, Not Stand-Alone

I seldom use the phrase "blended learning," mostly because it is redundant; I have never seen any learning that wasn't blended. Even text coming across a pager is blended with one's experience when it is actually used.

Nevertheless, the casual definition of blended learning has been using e-learning as a stand-alone set-up and support to the classroom's core learning. Again, simulations turn that model around. Because they are often challenging and require some hand-holding, successful deployments will instead *use classrooms as set-up and support* of a simulation's *core learning*.

7. World as It Is, Not Should Be

Most training organizations are politically correct, especially those aligned with corporate, rather than business units. Their output reflects a view of life that is multi-cultural, populated by equal numbers of males and females, ethical, has managers following rules, balanced between work and home, and in most ways fair. This was true of the training groups at Enron and WorldCom, as well as almost everywhere else.

But simulations that are politically correct, at the expense of accuracy, die on the vine. They are found out almost instantly. This seems obvious for product simulations (can you imagine building a model of a product that worked the way you would like it to, not how it actually performed?), but a surprisingly large number of managers who commission soft-skills simulations still want to portray a perfect world. Interestingly enough, one of the world's great advertising positions came out of rare corporate honesty (Avis: We're number two so we try harder), but that is another point.

That is not to say that a simulation cannot make an organization better. But one has to accurately model the culture, warts and all, and then reward behavior of the participant that reflects the higher ideals.

8. One "Level" at a Time

Look at Paramount's Star Trek games. While many of the games from the franchise have been terrible, quite a few have been really good.

Each of those top games did not try to capture the entire Star Trek experience. They instead focused on a narrow part of the whole experience. As with Charles and Ray Eames' classic *Power of Ten* movie, one can cycle through the different order of magnitude each of the games represents.

- In games such as Star Trek® Deep Space Nine®: The Fallen™ and Voyager™: Elite Force™ you play a single person running around huge space ships completing errands.

- In Bridge Commander™, you bump up a perspective and play a captain controlling these huge ships. You still play the game from a single person's perspective, but now you are controlling part of the ship directly, working with teammates who control the other aspects.

- You bump up another level in the Starfleet Command™ series, where you take hands-on control of the core workings of a large ship yourself, including power and weapons. You no longer have a voice or physical form.

- You bump up still another level in the Armada™ series. You control dozens of ships in battles in a section of space. You no longer have to worry about the minutia of ship operation, but instead resource gathering, strategy, and ship deployment.

- You can then go to the highest level in Birth of the Federation™. At this scale, even the ship battles are not your key focus, as you negotiate alliances, seize territory, and plan technology across the history of an empire.

The instinct for a simulation designer is to do everything. The discipline is to aim carefully, narrowly, and then go deep. These games did not do well *despite* how narrowly they focused, but *because* of how narrowly they focused.

9. Talent

I was talking to some U.S. Army personnel about hiring training people. These officers weren't asking about classroom instructors or curriculum builders; they were looking for level and sound designers, 2D and 3D artists, animators and modelers, and some lead engineers. Yes, it is a new world.

They are at the beginning of a five-year program to build and release game-like but educationally valid simulations to expose more people to their training programs. Their flagship simulation, America's Army: Operations, is available for free download to anyone starting Fourth of July, 2002.

As the Army is learning, hiring talent away from the game world is almost impossible. Their work is fun, well-paid, well-supported, and lower-risk, if not overly rewarding from a societal perspective.

10. CD-ROM/Hard Drive Versus Web Delivered

Is it better to use hard disks and processor power or a lot of bandwidth? Simulations that require hard disks and high processor power take more work to install but are low impact to any IT infrastructure after that. Simulations that require high bandwidth are Web delivered, which is easier to deploy up-front, but require huge network bandwidth during use. Multi-player games, especially with rich output models, still require significant bandwidth, even if they are installed on the client server.

11. Role of Standards

Right now, standards aren't even close to handling any of the emerging content types, including simulations. Likewise, LMSs have a hard time tracking them. It has been said that those who believe in Murphy's Law don't have a broad enough imagination. Likewise, those who believe in imminent standards don't have a broad enough view of e-learning.

Said Ed Glabus when he was president of MindSim Corporation, "SCORM seems to be gaining some momentum, but even the military, which not only is pushing SCORM, but also organizationally has standards to the nth degree, is having difficulty in creating a migration path for simulations."

11. Evaluation

It will be harder to evaluate simulation-based content. We have all learned how to skim presentations, skim books, skim magazine articles, and even skim the evening news. But you can't skim a simulation. It would be like trying to see all of Disney World in ten minutes. You may cover the ground, but you will not have the experience.

The harder issue is that the buyers from the HR or training department are often several computer generations away from the users. In the words of Marc Prensky, the buyers are "technology immigrants" and the users are often "technology native." What seems hard for the older people can be second-nature for the younger.

13. Price

Computer games are expensive to build. They will cost millions. So how much should an e-learning simulation cost? Prices range everywhere from $100 to $1,000 per user. Are they more similar to a book or a course?

14. Toolkits Pushed Instead of Finished Products

When the artificial intelligence boom of the early 1980s was in full swing, vendors were selling AI toolkits to large enterprises to build their own expert systems. Few enterprises did successfully, and all of the vendors went away. Venture capitalists love toolkits and are supporting companies today to push "simulation toolkits." These tend to force a limited cyclical and systems model, but let organizations put in some different linear content. Eventually toolkits will be popular, around (not across) genres, and not until successful simulation models have propagated.

15. Localization Is Difficult

Localization is the process of taking content developed for one country and making it useful in another country. The denser content is, the more expensive it is to localize. The flip side, though, is also true. Simulations will not number in the hundreds, but the tens, making the effort more manageable.

16. Do You Know What You Know?

It is harder to test simulation-learned material than it is to test text-book-learned material from traditional multiple-choice tests. As with life, people might learn different things.

17. "Gaming" Simulations

One fear about simulations is that people will learn how to "beat them," instead of learning from them.

This is an issue, but perhaps less so than it first seems. There are three stages of playing a game. First is utter frustration and misery. You fail immediately. You hate it. Then, when you get a bit more comfortable with the interface and metaphor, you buy into the illusion and have a great time. Finally, you get cynical and try to exploit the cracks. The third stage is when gaming happens. I hope in e-learning people won't be playing long enough that that happens, although it is always something to watch for.

Next Steps

The list is long, and daunting. But most of the items, especially around experience and expectations, that seem the hardest today will be absolutely commonplace in under ten years.

The other types of "problems," such as the difficulty of localization and the need to take learning sabbaticals, are worth noting, as they contrast with the premise of e-learning. But this premise, the dot-coming of content, will increasingly be attacked, and not just from simulations.

Rolling out content that does not need to be significantly localized or replacing training with bits of onscreen help are doable. But like a dog chasing the car, the bigger question is, Why would you want to?

Chapter Twenty-One

A Manifest Destiny

Simulations and the Training Industry

> Our goal is to use commercial off the shelf (COTS)
> equipment for simulations.
>
> —*Stephanie Lackey, Interdisciplinary/*
> *Computer Engineer, AIR—4962, NAVAIR, TSD*

I was trying to find the Ritz Carlton hotel in Kansas City. It was one in the morning, and it was raining hard. The plane had been delayed over eight hours, and I had missed a reception, but I still had to present the next day at a nearby pharmaceutical company.

Typically, I was lost. I could not make out any of the milestones. There is a slight chance that I was swearing. I was certainly in no mood for serendipitous learning.

Then I saw the road. My heart jumped. I double-checked with my scrawled notes. They matched. I turned sharply to the right. Luckily, there was no car behind me (but then, it was ONE IN THE MORNING in KANSAS CITY). And I drove up the little hill. There was the sign for the hotel. It looked beautiful. I pulled in. I got out of the car, relieved, exhausted, and now fretting about finalizing the next day's presentation.

The doorman signaled to me. I walked over. He pointed out that one of my tires was almost out of air. The car was sagging to the right. My heart dropped.

The doorman then did something to earn him a hallowed place in my own hall of honor. He told me he would take care it. Being from the New York area, I view all nice people as either simple or insane. But I was too tired to do anything else. He took my rental car keys and sent me on my way. The next morning, I had a new car from Hertz sitting in my spot. A bag that I had forgotten about had been transferred. There was even a $25 Hertz certificate sitting in my passenger seat.

There is an excitement being around skilled people. It frees us up to do our jobs, comfortable that others are doing theirs.

I feel it when sitting around a table at the Pentagon listening to people in the military talking about operations. They understand and support each other's processes, while focusing their disagreement on the relevant areas.

I get the same feeling talking to L.L. Bean's customer representatives. They often have first-hand experience with the products they are discussing. They can tell you how many of an item is in stock.

I have the same feel from Disney World employees. I can even get that feeling of skill going into a Wal-Mart.

These people approach their days confidently. They have training, plus experience, plus vision. They have mastered various paradoxes:

- They have both consistency and flexibility.
- They are knowledgeable, and they know where to turn for help.
- They know the rules and know when to break them (one of my favorite quotes is "A gentleman is never rude unintentionally").

Contrast that to the places without skilled employees.

You know in a moment when you are talking to an employee who doesn't have a clue. You get that sinking feeling. They use rules as a crutch ("Let me tell you why you can't do it"). Or they just look at you blankly. Or they shake their heads a lot.

A Management Issue

This is not just a line-worker issue. In fact, proportionately, and in relationship to their actual jobs, management is less skilled than any other part of an organization.

Most organizations have very limited management training. The bandied-about reason for this, what the training people will say, is that most managers do not ask for it because they are embarrassed at what they don't know. While this is a bit true, and certainly depends on the culture, the bigger issue is more relevant. *Most management skills cannot be taught through a linear experience, such as a classroom.* Managers have a justified lack of faith in a training department's ability to teach anything but process skills.

Scott Adams' popular syndicated strip "Dilbert" accurately portrays the huffing and bluffing of so many teams of corporate management. They often mistake involvement in past successes for skill, living in fear of getting caught.

The bigger scandal is the amount of dishonesty. Because I spent a few years at the highest level of several organizations, below the radar of many of the people by whom I was surrounded, I saw a lot of dirty tricks.

Some dirty tricks were subtle. Everyone instinctively grabbed credit for successes and distanced themselves from failures. Some people were strategically left off or put on distribution lists (in both memos and emails). I have seen some projects staffed with people who were essentially politically appointees to keep tabs on potential internal competitors.

Other dirty tricks were more blatant. I have seen people give colleagues wrong information about a meeting. I have seen people invite an internal competitor to a meeting, but not tell him that he was on the agenda and was to present. Imagine his surprise when he got up in front of a group unprepared. I have seen people not invite a rival to a meeting or conference call to which she should be invited. Some people play hardball with who controls an account. Budgets are cut from strategic growth businesses to cover up failures in traditional businesses. I have seen guiltless people singled out and fired as penance, to prove action had been taken for a larger failure.

I saw a director listen as his direct reports presented a business plan, trash the plan in front of them, present the plan to his boss as his work without changing a word, have the plan approved, and then fire all of the people who originally created the plan to get rid of the witnesses.

Of course, these involve moral issues. But every one of these was the result of people in over their heads. Managers so often do not have the skills they need to do their jobs.

Training for all parts of an organization will have to be a massive part of the solution. The irony so far has been that traditional e-learning, while increasing the range of training professionals, actually reduced their strategic impact by limiting them to teaching only highly linear/process skills. We have to do better.

The Last Great Training Initiative

The last time this level of enterprise competence was deliberately developed was during the "Quality" movement. It was a stunning, if focused, success.

Previously, quality had meant anything that was expensive. Cadillacs were considered quality. So were Rolexes and Mont Blanc pens. Disposable pens were not. Quality was a concept that was warm, fuzzy, easy to understand, and, from a business sense, utterly useless.

Then something happened in the early 1980s. Instead of meaning "high end," a few manufacturers redefined quality to mean "meeting the needs of the customer." And customers could be either internal or external. Total Quality Management (TQM) was born.

Incredibly, when companies from around the world came together to talk about quality, they were talking about the same thing. They could learn from each other on how to solve implementation problems.

The knowledge base around quality deepened quickly. Product designers had to start listening to customers. Consistency across a manufacturing process became critical, spawning the discipline of Six Sigma. Speed became king, prompting work into A *delta* T.

Quality was strongly supported (and strongly invested in) by managers, CEOs, even U.S. Presidents. The highest potential people, rather than the staffers, were put in charge of the programs.

It saved more than a few manufacturing organizations. And it remains healthy today.

A Dozen Quality Movements?

But "quality" is just one program. People who run groups and organizations need a dozen disciplines, equally critical to an organization. Most managers should focus on developing at least one key "quality level" skill every year for as long as they are working.

High-priced B-school executive programs are great for prestige, fabulous to make contact for job switching and recruiting, a nice sabbatical to get perspective on work, and even a great reward, but are too limited in capacity, too expensive, too inconsistent, and ultimately too disconnected from the real world.

Simulations will be the primary vehicles for this type of focused up-skilling (although it will be heavily augmented from other advanced e-learning-enabled models, including skunkworks projects, microcosms, apprenticeships, comprehensive help desks (including expert-level help). And the skills delivered will be much more powerful than quality, because simulations and other advanced models support *open-ended* and *cyclical* skills, not just *linear* skills. (Quality was a process skill, which is why it did not transfer to the service industries.) Managers will finally become consistently skilled in managing change, sales, financials, legal, communication, project management, employees, and so many more.

Some organizations will roll out massive, consistent simulation-based programs tied to strategic initiatives. Others will tailor them specifically for each employee.

The top organizations will relish the opportunity to raise the level of competence and intelligent discourse. They will role model adoption for the rest of us.

New Content Plus New Delivery Equals New Genres

The training world (both internal employees and vendors) will have to fulfill this. No one else can do it.

Given that, it is the *manifest destiny of e-learning to establish ten to twenty examples of education genres*. Against the ever-growing informal competition with the training departments for ways of learning, such as chat rooms, messenger tools, Google™, and even vendor-sponsored "free" magazines, these formal, dynamic, consistent, educational experiences will be the "trim tab" for the entire organization and the point of highest, differentiated value for training professionals.

Virtual Leader is an example of an interpersonal genre, using leadership as the current "mod." We will see other simulations, equally deep, in the areas of accounting, project management, time management, reorganizations, change management, sourcing and supply change, negotiating, sexual harassment/ethics/safety, and even renewal and adaptation.

Creating this core curriculum of simulations, however, will not be easy. During the first decade of the new millennia, simulation designers will continue forging ahead in uncharted territory.

They will have to create new genres of educational contents, as with Virtual Leader, that both present new approaches to content (focusing on systems and open-ended environments) and new ways of delivering it (focusing on interface, muscle memory, and cyclical content). Either side of the equation is daunting; accomplishing both is a medium-size miracle. System-based content without an interface that takes advantage of cyclical content will be inapplicable. A perfect interface without the content will not teach much of value.

Organizations are being established, mostly through nonprofit channels, that are "studying" and trying to articulate this future content. The problem is that they tend to be heavily impacted by academic "lifers," which limit their chances of success, or by private-sector analysts, such as in my old job.

These efforts are mostly doomed. The need today is to create forward, not study backward. Most people with Ph.D. after their names will find it too hard to unlearn what they have spent years learning in order to make themselves relevant to either the open-ended/systems or the interface/relevancy side. They will want to create content about history, mostly their own.

Innovative *for-profit organizations*, and *students* chaffing against their academic environments, will more likely develop this future content. I suspect college dropouts will be the single greatest creative and influential force here (enraging all of the teachers who failed them), building content in their basements and in their spare time. The hardest part, I believe, will be creating the right interface to teach cyclical skills. Finding the right model to make a skill transferable is very tricky.

And even then, pioneers will receive uneven rewards for their work. Some new genres will die quickly. They will not contain the perfect blend of elements—linear, cyclical, and open-ended. Some genres will be ahead of their times and will be seeds for others to nourish later on.

But others will be brilliant immediately. They will thrive, endure, and be improved on for decades. These creative rebels will (ironically) present the rules for the next generations of designers. We will have models of educational simulations just as surely and specifically as we have models for news shows, situation comedies, and talk shows that were created by the rebels of the last generation.

This will take years. Then, and only then, can training departments buy and modify, and occasionally build their own, educational simulations. By intelligently deploying these, well-supported with other types of content, training departments will finally be a critical part of an organization at the highest levels.

And we will all spend more time in the company of skilled employees, both as colleagues, employees, managers, and customers. I can't wait.

Epilogue: Looking Back at Schools

> Unless a technology investment is clearly linked
> to a defined behavior change, it will go off-track
> sooner or later. The behavioral change must be
> measurable and directly linked to a strategic change
> goal of the organization.
> — *Andy Snider, President, Snider Associates*

The development and adoption of simulations will change the nature of work, change the skill sets of our culture, and create an international industry that will eventually account for billions in revenue. It will lead to new research projects and force the rethinking of traditional content to make it more useful. One of the greatest impacts will be on the schools for our youngest citizens.

Our Greatest Challenge

Improving schools internationally is the greatest challenge of our generation. The way we operate them is the root problem of so many other issues, from obesity to terrorism to the degradation of the environment.

As is appropriate for the task, some of our country's greatest leaders have tried to tackle the education issue. Here is a partial listing.

There is David Kearns. While at Xerox he turned a crumbling copier company into a world-class business, pioneering the quality movement in the process. He wrote *Winning the Brain Race: A Bold Plan to Make Our Schools Competitive*. He was, from 1991 until 1993, the deputy secretary of the U.S. Department of Education, and he recently taught at the Harvard Graduate School of Education.

There is George Lucas, a person who is on target to pull off a tightly organized, financially staggering nine-movie "trilogy of trilogies," an organizational, creative, technical, and business challenge that dwarfs smaller tasks like running a country. The technology and innovations that pour out of him in tangential areas (such as THX) would define him if his *Star Wars* epics did not. He is the founder of The George Lucas Educational Foundation (GLEF), which published *Edutopia: Success Stories for Learning in the Digital Age*. He is also the founder of Lucas Learning, to provide K-12 classrooms technology-based instructional materials that make learning challenging, engaging, and fun. Some titles that Lucas Learning has put out include: Star Wars® Yoda's Challenge™ Activity Center, Star Wars® Math: Jabba's Game Galaxy™, Star Wars®: The Gungan Frontier™, Star Wars®: DroidWorks®, Star Wars® Pit Droids®.

There is Lou Gerstner, another re-invigorator of a little enterprise called IBM. As well as saving Big Blue, from 1996 to 2002 he co-chaired Achieve, an organization created by U.S. governors and business leaders to drive high academic standards for public schools in the United States. He is co-author of the book *Reinventing Education: Entrepreneurship in America's Public Schools*. Of the thirty-seven major speeches he delivered between 1995 and 2001, fully eight were on education reform (the others being to shareholders and on broader technology issues).

There is Michael Milken. In 1982 he co-founded and endowed the Milken Family Foundation, which has been a leading force for advancing education, youth programs, inner city solutions, AIDS research, pediatric neurology, and various forms of cancer. He is also the chairman of Knowledge Universe, the parent corporation for companies focusing on people development such as UNext, LeapFrog, k12, Knowledge Learning Corp., Productivity Point International, TEC Worldwide, and KnowledgePlanet.

And recently, former GE chairman Jack Welch has entered the club. He has partnered with New York schools to teach leadership to principals. I suspect his involvement will increase.

All are brilliant, successful, staggeringly competent individuals—and there are others, taking on schools or partnering with them to change the way our teachers teach and children learn. But are they laying a new foundation that will change education over years, or are they Napoleons trying to invade/reform Russia, or Don Quixotes tilting at illusory foes? Are they challenging enough fundamental assumptions about schools, including *what* to teach, as well as *how* to teach it, to really make a difference?

Beyond Linear Content

One place to start is to look at content that we are currently teaching. Anyone looking at simulations is used to looking at all three types: cyclical, linear, and systems. Schools deliberately teach linear content. They teach history and literature and math. But they accidentally teach cyclical and systems content as well, and that may be negating much of their benefit.

Non-Transferable Cyclical Skills

Every day, in every class, and with every assignment, students learn cyclical skills. These are the highly precise skills they learn through constant repetition. The skills are much more enduring than our memory of the date of a war or the food habits of a bat. Here are some examples of the types of cyclical content that schools teach:

- How to be called by the teacher when you know the answer;
- How not to be called by the teacher when you do not know the answer;
- How to cram for a test;
- How to write a term paper;
- How to be the first to answer all of the easy questions;
- How and when to offer to help, such as hand out worksheets, erase blackboards, or clean the room;
- How and when to compliment the teacher's clothing;

- How and when to ask for extra help to feign interest;
- When to make eye contact when listening to a teacher;
- How and when to keep desk neat;
- How to draw in notebook when pretending to take notes;
- How to pass notes/speak to classmates without being detected;
- How to obtain very good snacks/lunch;
- How and when to do busywork, such as keeping desk neat, straightening up work areas; and
- How and when to intensely observe classmates without getting caught.

Given that these are the applied skills learned, it is no wonder students are so out of place in any "real setting." They have the wrong "muscle memory."

An Inwardly Focused System

Schools also teach students a tremendous amount about the system that they are in. While exaggerated for dramatic effect, John Taylor Gatto, the New York State Teacher of the Year in 1991, summed up that there are only six lessons he really taught in school:

- The first lesson I teach is: "Stay in the class where you belong."
- The second lesson I teach you is to turn on and off like a light switch.
- The third lesson I teach you is to surrender your will to a predestined chain of command.
- The fourth lesson I teach is that only I determine what curriculum you will study.
- In lesson five I teach that your self-respect should depend on an observer's measure of your worth.
- In lesson six I teach you that you are being watched.

The way that students learn these six lessons is open-ended—they all do it differently. Some will learn by asking a wrong question. Some will learn by overhearing conversations between teachers. Some will learn by trying to do one project over another. But they all end up with a similar understanding of the system around them.

The Two-Fold Role of Simulation

Simulations, as discussed, can directly add valuable cyclical and systems content. They can teach at these levels to tap so much more of students' capabilities. The transformation in experience will be as rich and dramatic as going from watching black and white movies to watching color movies.

By rounding out content, simulations can positively impact the negative system that Gatto describes. But can they completely overturn it? Indirectly, I believe they can.

The Challenge of Alignment

A major root cause for Gatto's observation is a lack of alignment between most schools and the rest of the world. Here is a one-hour exercise that anyone can do to judge any educational institution's alignment level. Ready?

Look at Lunchtime

Go to the school at noon and have lunch.

There. You are finished.

A one question quiz: Did the students eat well? In far too many situations, the answer is, "Not at all." Those are the schools with the lowest alignment.

Why does that matter, you may ask? School food is some outsourced function, not a core competency.

I disagree. Lunch says far too much about a school.

- Students care about food. It is a major theme of conversations and bartering.
- Parents care about food.
- Food drives short-term performance. Better food means better learning that day.
- Food drives long-term health. Better food means healthier people.
- Obesity is a national epidemic.
- Eating well is a critical habit for gaining control over your life.
- Research guides our understanding of food and the effect of food, which changes over time.
- Preparing good food is difficult.

Institutionally, not caring about food is not being aligned. And nutrition is an apt microcosm for all content. At the deepest process level, schools handle learning similarly to the way they handle nutrition.

The Challenge of Alignment

Unaligned processes are not just accidental. Schools are inwardly focused. They don't reach out to parents, children, the landowners who pay their salaries, the politicians, or the businesses. Schools have had to learn to keep distance because they know that most sane, practical truism of all: *What is taught is governed by what can be taught*.

Schools have stayed away from listening because they know that, when they do listen, they are asked to teach non-linear skills. Principals and superintendents are asked to teach project management, interpersonal skills, teamwork, analysis, leadership, speaking, and nutrition.

And these they would be unable to deliver using their traditional techniques. Any attempts at alignment would open up a

Pandora's box that would simply frustrate everyone without a solution in sight. Schools have had to learn to stop listening.

With new scalable learning techniques aimed at cyclical, linear, and systems skills, school reform is possible. As simulations are explored, schools will finally be able to do what they want—and need—to do.

It is true that schools will not be the originators of simulation-based content. They will subtly fight it and set it up to fail. They will compare it narrowly to traditional content, and find it wanting. But once the right simulation genres exist, and schools finally adopt them, the change in the very nature of schools will be extraordinary. We will envy our children for their experience, and they will better teach us.

Glossary

ADL—An e-learning standard.

AICC—An e-learning standard.

Artificial intelligence—The ability of a computer to behave in some aspect the way a human behaves.

Application Service Provider (ASP)—While many applications such as word processors or databases reside on a client (a personal computer) or a server (a computer within an enterprise's firewalls), some exist at a vendor's location and are accessed through the Internet. This Internet access model is called ASP, or "hosted." For example, according to research firm IDC, the majority (64.9 percent) of LMSs still reside on customer servers. The trend over the past two years, however, with ASP systems taking significant share away from installed systems, is likely to continue.

Asynchronous e-learning—Content that does not involve other people's live participation. Most asynchronous e-learning is based on workbooks that have been made into web pages.

Avatar—Any onscreen character. It is a term used mostly in academic circles.

Bandwidth—A measure of how much information per unit of time a network connection can deliver. In an enterprise environment, such as a corporation, bandwidth has to be shared. Therefore an e-learning application that has a high bandwidth requirement will actually slow down other business critical operations.

Blended learning models—A term first used by dot-com publisher Brandon Hall, blended models suggest that the best learning happens when multiple learning techniques are employed, including e-learning and traditional learning. The more philosophical question might be: Is there such a thing as unblended learning?

Bot—See non-playing character.

Broadband—Very fast network access. Also known as "thick pipes."

Computer game—Any computer application engaged solely or primarily for entertainment. The computer game industry will probably earn almost $10 billion in revenues in 2003.

Content—There are many different types of e-learning content. Most content is delivered directly to the end-learners to make them more productive. Successful programs will involve more than one type of content.

The two common styles of e-learning content are workbook-style Web pages, either specifically built for an organization or generic, and virtual classroom sessions.

e-Learning also involves administrative content. There are curricula, including skills maps, which list, suggest, demand, or even prohibit courses for end-learners. Administrative content also includes records of who took what courses and how they did.

Cyclical content—Formal content that develops "muscle memory." In the case of a simulation, this happens at the interface level. If the interface does not line up with the a real task, the transferability of skills will be insignificant.

Easter egg—Hidden pieces of content only available to those who are told or can figure out how to reach them.

e-Learning integrator—Many consulting organizations have entered into e-learning with the value proposition of applying the right e-learning solution to a given business problem, determining what to measure, and managing third-party software. Their opportunity is enormous, as CEOs begin caring more about formal learning programs.

For traditional consulting organizations, however, the reality is tougher, because the e-learning competencies in most consulting companies are highly fragmented. Some large companies have been approached by different parts of the same consulting company to handle e-learning. Currently, I count seven groups covering e-learning in a typical large consulting company.

The ERP (enterprise resource planner) practices have been the longest users of e-learning to support the training for their implementations, usually sold as a percent of total implementation (around 5 percent). Some are even moving into the LMS vendor arena and pushing an LMS solution as another module and an extension of the HR solution (like PeopleSoft).

The internal training people have been automating their courses and wanting to sell them externally, selling on a course per student model (around $100 to $1,000 per student).

The BPR (business process re-engineering) people have been selling e-learning as a support tool, a line item in a much larger contract.

The external e-business people have been developing e-learning as a value-added tool for their clients' sites on a daily cost-plus basis.

The internal e-business people have been developing e-learning from scratch as an extension to their other offerings to sell to their clients and B2C, often sold on a per-student population subscription model.

The knowledge management practices view e-learning as an extension of their offerings and are charging for maintaining the infrastructure.

Systems integrators sell the integration of off-the-shelf learning components.

e-Learning—e-Learning is a broad combination of processes, content, and infrastructure to use computers and networks to scale and/or improve one or more significant parts of a learning value chain, including management and delivery. Originally aimed at lowering cost while increasing accessibility and for measurability of employees, e-learning is increasingly being used to include advanced learning techniques such as simulators and communities of practice and to include customers and vendors as well.

e-Learning portal—At the simplest level, the portal provides end-learners with a verification process, a list of courses they can or should take, and links to sign up for or launch the appropriate learning event. The LMSs typically manage the portal.

Portal integration is expanding in at least two different directions:

Within e-learning, portals are increasingly being able to launch an e-learning event without leaving the portal wrapper. For example, virtual classrooms and chat rooms can be initiated within a smaller window in the portal page.

Outside of e-learning, portals are becoming more universal. In some organizations, learning data has to be imported into a third-party portal where it is only one of many features. Therefore, e-learning choices, as with other portal-based services, will increasingly be influenced by the Microsoft.NET versus Java 2 Platform, Enterprise Edition (J2EE), debate.

First-person shooters—A highly successful computer game genre that puts the player vantage behind the barrel of a weapon. The genre stresses a priority on fast decision making over complicated, open-ended strategy.

Game—An interactive and entertaining source of play, sometimes used to learn a lesson.

Gameplay—The combination of cyclical, linear, and open-ended content, and other elements, that makes a computer game addictive.

Graphic engine—The software applications that convert computer code into three-dimensional-looking images on a screen. Once, every game had a unique proprietary graphic engine. Increasingly, in part due to the cost and timeframe of development, third-party graphic engines are licensed to game developers. Graphic engines tend to be built and optimized around a given game genre. Common metrics around graphic engines are the number of polygons they can present on the screen at a time at a given frames-per-second rate. LithTech, Doom, and Quake are three popular engine brands.

Interface—The way a person engages a computer application at the cyclical level.

Knowledge management—Knowledge management, like artificial intelligence, describes a problem, not a solution. The issue of managing even half of an organization's intellectual assets will never be solved in my lifetime. Even the best systems shoot for percents in the single digit.

Most knowledge management systems are also text-based. And one of the few similarities among subject-matter experts is that they hate writing. Writing takes a lot of time and skill, and many ideas don't survive the journey. Most experts instead have built rich skills around talking and gesturing, in part because they provides emotional as well as intellectual range.

Learning content management system (LCMS)—Learning management systems failed to sufficiently manage learning content, so a new class of tools, learning content management systems (LCMS), emerged. These content management systems gave enterprises and vendors the ability to parse courses into smaller and smaller pieces, starting the industry down a path that would eventually break down many of the barriers between the disciplines of e-learning and knowledge management.

Learning community—A theoretical cluster of people who view part of their ongoing role as providing useful information to others in the cluster.

Linear content—Content that is either minimally or non-interactive. DVDs, with branching and added features, represent the highest form of pure linear content. Within a simulation, pre-rendered scenes or even most dialogue quotes are linear. If the simulation does not provide adequate linear content, the users will be lost and/or not care.

Learning management systems (LMS)—Learning management systems (LMSs) have two primary goals: to get the right content to the right person at the right time and to record and report the event. This functionality is critical to the management of any training organization.

Beyond that, LMSs can be responsible for integrating and optimizing different learning channels and vendors, keeping track of costs, allowing end-learners to search for content among all options, and contributing to a successful skills management program.

Massively multi-player role-playing games (MMORPGs)—Persistent computer environments occupied by both player and computer-controlled characters. Humans pay between $7 and $15 a month for access to these worlds. While gathering momentum through 2002, the market is likely to be littered by failures through the summer of 2003. Everquest has defined the market.

Non-playing character (bot)—An onscreen character that is controlled by the computer.

Open ended content—A system that the user can engage and understand through nearly infinite different paths. If the simulation does not provide a relevant, dynamic, systems model that can be engaged from multiple angles, the learning will be trivial.

Platform games—A computer game genre in which a character navigates a primarily one-dimensional space, reacting to oncoming obstacles. Donkey Kong® was an early and popular example of this genre. It stresses pure reactive, cyclical skills.

Real-time strategy games (RTS)—A computer game genre in which a player is a disembodied leader of an invasion force, weighing the collection of raw materials, research, the construction of offensive and defensive capabilities, and maneuvers. The genre stresses a balance between complicated, open-ended strategy and cyclical, fast decision making.

Role-playing games—A computer game genre in which a player is a single character or team of characters in a maze or otherwise simulated world. The player decides how the character's or team's skills and capabilities evolve over the course of the experience, for example, choosing between stealth and firepower, defensive and offensive, and ranged and close striking ability. The genre stresses a balance between complicated, open-ended strategy and fast decision making.

SCORM—An e-learning standard. It has been pushed by the military, but so far cannot adequately track simulations (which are also pushed by the military).

Set—The relatively static environment where most television shows and computer games take place. While sitcom television sets don't have ceilings, most computer game sets do.

Simulation—Tools that allow users to learn by practicing in a repeatable, focused environment. Gartner states, "Simulation software has been used in equipment service and military applications since the 1980s" and "Simulation will evolve to become the 'killer application' for e-learning."

To quote Don Morrison from his book, *E-Learning Strategies*, "In the past, what passed for e-learning simulations were no more than simulations of simulations—elaborately constructed exercises in branching that gave the learner the impression anything could happen when in reality all outcomes had been scripted in advance of the learning event. e-Learning developers are starting to build authentic simulations based on rules engines and vast databases. These simulations contain an almost infinite number of variables. No one—not even the author—can predict all outcomes."

These authentic simulations will be CD-ROM delivered, using Microsoft's DirectX as an API, and require computers that have graphic cards.

Gartner writes: "Enterprises should evaluate where simulation can supplement and enhance their most-critical learning environments."

State-based calculation model—An early simulation model with a limited number of options that tends to be turn based and backtrackable.

Streaming media—A technology model where video or audio is downloaded at rates comparable to its presentation to the user. Because pure streaming is difficult given the inconsistency of the Internet, the hard disk of a computer is often used as a buffer. Higher density content such as video requires more powerful networks.

Synchronous e-learning—Virtual classroom (a.k.a. live e-learning or synchronous e-learning) tools provide an infrastructure for synchronous (same time, different location) courses integrating voices, slides, and application sharing, as well as an authoring tool for capturing and editing sessions for future use.

They can be used for intimate problem-solving conversations, a CEO speech to a company, a sales seminar to one hundred perspectives, or a virtual keynote at a conference.

Virtual classroom experiences have a very high customer satisfaction, predictably higher than asynchronous.

Third-person shooters—A game genre very similar to first-person shooters, but instead of seeing the world through the eyes of the central character, the player can see the central character. This genre stresses character development and physical actions such as jumping and hiding more than does first-person. Popular examples are Tomb Raider™ and Splinter Cell™.

Trigger—In a computer-generated environment, a predictable, discontinuous response to a predetermined continuous event.

For example, after attracting the one thousandth visitor to your amusement park, you may get a cash influx of $1M.

Turn-based strategy games—A game genre wherein a player controls a very complicated system. The genre stresses open-ended gameplay over cyclical skills. Popular examples included the Civilization series and Sid Meier's Alpha Centauri.

Raw Leadership Content

The mind can be programmed to help solve problems, to enhance insight, intuition, and inspiration. All you have to do to access this part of your brain is to relax. Don't force creativity, coax it. Mindless activities like exercise, driving, and even watching television are great idea generators. Many people get their best ideas in the shower or just as they fall asleep. The key is to get into the right state of mind—the state of relaxation.

> —*Barry Goldsmith, CEO, Goldsmith Consulting,*
> *Quoted in* Los Angeles Business Journal, *August 28, 2001*

Bring humor into the workplace where possible. Laughing eases tension and stress and reduces anxiety levels. It also makes for a more personalized work atmosphere.

> —*Bob Adams,* The Everything Leadership, *2001*

Strategic intent aims to create employee excitement, not just employee satisfaction. The more excited a worker is, the less are remuneration and hygiene the sole barometer of contentment.

> —*Gary Hamel and C.K. Prahalad,* Competing for the Future, *p. 135*

Leadership is action, not position.

> —*Donald H. McGannon*

The best way to have a good idea is to have a lot of ideas.

> —*Dr. Linus Pauling*

In the movie *The Candidate*, Robert Redford wins election and famously asks, "What do we do now?"

  —*David R. Gergen*, Eyewitness to Power:
   The Essence of Leadership, Nixon to Clinton, *p. 171*

Reagan was as good that day as he had ever been in meetings. He stayed above the forest of facts we had provided and focused on the larger goals he wanted to pursue.

  —*David R. Gergen*, Eyewitness to Power:
   The Essence of Leadership, Nixon to Clinton, *p. 153*

Had Roosevelt and Churchill not rallied the Western democracies, civilization might have perished.

  —*David R. Gergen*, Eyewitness to Power:
   The Essence of Leadership, Nixon to Clinton, *p. 12*

Nixon liked a diversity of voices on his staff.

  —*David R. Gergen*, Eyewitness to Power:
   The Essence of Leadership, Nixon to Clinton, *p. 23*

The main reasons CEOs fail is not mistakes in strategy or finance but simple inability to execute—to get done what they wanted to get done.

  —*Geoffery Colvin*, Fortune, *December 10, 2001*

The boss may have the power to fire workers and injure the worker's record, but the boss, by the imposition of power, can never force his employee to work to his capacity or to create.

  —*Gerry L. Spence*, How to Argue and Win Every Time:
   At Home, at Work, in Court, Everywhere, Every Day, *p. 42*

Fear is painful. I hate its frequent companionship. Yet it challenges me. It energizes my senses.

  —*Gerry L. Spence*, How to Argue and Win Every Time:
   At Home, at Work, in Court, Everywhere, Every Day, *p. 14*

If I were required to choose the single essential skill from the many that make up the art of the argument, it would be the ability to listen.

> —*Gerry L. Spence*, How to Argue and Win Every Time:
> At Home, at Work, in Court, Everywhere, Every Day, *p. 67*

Many in positions of power take up such posts in the fulfillment of a neurotic need to exercise power over others.

> —*Gerry L. Spence*, How to Argue and Win Every Time:
> At Home, at Work, in Court, Everywhere, Every Day, *p. 43*

IBM wanted a capable businessman with fresh ideas.

> —*Doug Garr*, IBM Redux: Lou Gerstner and
> the Business Turnaround of the Decade, *p. 25*

Gerstner suspected that IBM had lost its competitive edge because it was slow to market.

> —*Doug Garr*, IBM Redux: Lou Gerstner and
> the Business Turnaround of the Decade, *p. 70*

Gerstner vowed to "seek to create brilliant strategies and execute them brilliantly."

> —*Doug Garr*, IBM Redux: Lou Gerstner and
> the Business Turnaround of the Decade, *p. 29*

Already intellectually drained and bankrupt of ideas, [IBM] was now leaderless and rudderless.

> —*Doug Garr*, IBM Redux: Lou Gerstner and
> the Business Turnaround of the Decade, *p. 20*

A "deliverable" was a tangible short-term assignment with an inviolable deadline.

> —*Doug Garr*, IBM Redux: Lou Gerstner and
> the Business Turnaround of the Decade, *p. 97*

It was refreshing to many IBMers that Gerstner actually read their messages.

> *—Doug Garr,* IBM Redux: Lou Gerstner and
> the Business Turnaround of the Decade, *p. 35*

Gerstner did a lot of listening, not just to customers, but to the legions of analysts and technology pundits.

> *—Doug Garr,* IBM Redux: Lou Gerstner and
> the Business Turnaround of the Decade, *p. 59*

York divided people into two categories: those who got the job done and those who didn't.

> *—Doug Garr,* IBM Redux: Lou Gerstner and
> the Business Turnaround of the Decade, *p. 51*

Gerstner tried to shake up AMEX managers.

> *—Doug Garr,* IBM Redux: Lou Gerstner and
> the Business Turnaround of the Decade, *p. 96*

Czarnecki was just a very nice guy, too nice for the new IBM.

> *—Doug Garr,* IBM Redux: Lou Gerstner and
> the Business Turnaround of the Decade, *p. 53*

Maybe if they threw a few swears around, they could jump-start some somnolent brains.

> *—Doug Garr,* IBM Redux: Lou Gerstner and
> the Business Turnaround of the Decade, *p. 45*

Because our five-person office in Detroit was competing against DuPont's forty-person office, we had to be faster and more creative.

> *—Jack Welch,* Jack: Straight from the Gut, *p. 41*

Bob . . . had a million ideas and brought new life to the position.

> *—Jack Welch,* Jack: Straight from the Gut, *p. 47*

All of us were earthy, without pretense or formality—always blunt.
>—*Jack Welch*, Jack: Straight from the Gut, *p. 52*

I was really looking for people who were filled with passion and a desire to get things done.
>—*Jack Welch*, Jack: Straight from the Gut, *p. 54*

[The intellectuals] often turned out to be unfocused dabblers, unwilling to commit, lacking intensity and passion for any one thing.
>—*Jack Welch*, Jack: Straight from the Gut, *p. 54*

All leadership is influence.
>—*John C. Maxwell, Injoy, Inc.*

You're always more creative when relaxed.
>—*Lighthousewriters.com*

There is nothing like the sight of the gallows to clear the mind.
>—*Gary Tooker, Motorola, Inc.*

One of the shortcomings of American corporations is that they have focused far too much on good strategy and not nearly enough on good implementation.
>—*David T. Kearns,* Prophets in the Dark: How Xerox
>Reinvented Itself and Beat Back the Japanese, *p. 278*

Rickard knew that if the quality program was going to get anyplace in the organization he would have to place on the support of the princes and to dance past the kings.
>—*David T. Kearns,* Prophets in the Dark: How Xerox
>Reinvented Itself and Beat Back the Japanese, *p. 172*

If I participate in creating the change, I'm going to understand it better, and I am going to have ownership.
>—*David T. Kearns,* Prophets in the Dark: How Xerox
>Reinvented Itself and Beat Back the Japanese, *p. 280*

You can't wait around until everyone feels pain from the marketplace, because then it's too late. So you need to use some induced pain. You have to throw a few punches here and there.

> —David T. Kearns, Prophets in the Dark: How Xerox
> Reinvented Itself and Beat Back the Japanese, p. 280

The word "trust" appears in virtually every current book on leadership, and it is taken as a commonplace that without trust, leadership is impossible. . . ."

> —Robert C. Solomon

Write up your idea in a memo. People may roll their eyes if you bring a written handout, but at least there won't be any doubt as to whose it is.

> —Sarah Myers McGinty, Ph.D., quoted by Anne Fisher, Fortune, 2001

Knowing ignorance is strength. Ignoring knowledge is sickness.

> —Lao Tsu, Tao Te Ching, translated by
> Gia-Fu Feng Jane English, and Gis-Fu Feng, Section 71

How do we go about changing a culture that involves thousands of people, most of whom, from a distance, seem quite satisfied with things the way they are?

> —Peter Block, The Empowered Manager:
> Positive Political Skills at Work, p. xvii

Demand commitment instead of sacrifice.

> —Peter Block, The Empowered Manager:
> Positive Political Skills at Work, p. 75

The patriarchal belief is that self-restraint is essential to building a strong organization. . . . The price we pay for this attitude is that we put a cap on the well of people's motivation and passion and caring.

> —Peter Block, The Empowered Manager:
> Positive Political Skills at Work, p. 71

With so much change and turbulence taking place, people need leaders more than ever. Yet, with so many acquisitions, spin-offs, and launches taking place, people insist on maintaining their independence more than ever. And with so much decentralization and delayering of companies taking place, people struggle even to know what leadership is more than ever.

> —*The Founding Editors*, Fast Company, 1999

The creation of vision comes from a considerable amount of exploring, analyzing, and rooting around in the territory of the problem.

> —*Eliza G.C. Collins and Mary Anne Devanna*,
> The New Portable MBA, *p. 54*

Sometimes those who refuse to cooperate actually have valuable knowledge or abilities; they may even be indispensable to your success.

> —*Eliza G.C. Collins and Mary Anne Devanna*,
> The New Portable MBA, *p. 33*

Even direct subordinates may resist your orders when they are convinced you are wrong and will certainly drag their heels if they are afraid of proposed changes. . . . Fewer and fewer decisions can be made or implemented in isolation in the modern business organization.

> —*Eliza G.C. Collins and Mary Anne Devanna*,
> The New Portable MBA, *p. 33*

The capacity of any president to lead depends on focusing the nation's political attention and energies on two or three top priorities.

> —*Hedrick Smith*, The Power Game: How Washington Works, *p. 333*

The agenda game must be won first.

> —*Hedrick Smith*, The Power Game: How Washington Works, *p. 333*

No president can succeed unless he can build a governing coalition.

> —*Hedrick Smith*, The Power Game: How Washington Works, *p. 453*

Strike quickly for a win, during the early rush of power. That helps establish momentum and an aura of success.
—*Hedrick Smith*, The Power Game: How Washington Works, *p. 456*

Winning is power.
—*Hedrick Smith*, The Power Game: How Washington Works, *p. 456*

Horse-trading is the way the battle is fought in the final clinches.
—*Hedrick Smith*, The Power Game: How Washington Works, *p. 477*

Jack Kennedy . . . was the first successful presidential candidate to rely on personal appeal . . . to win the top prize.
—*Hedrick Smith*, The Power Game: How Washington Works, *p. 694*

To be a player is to have power or influence on some issue.
—*Hedrick Smith*, The Power Game: How Washington Works, *p. xiii*

One political party, for example, can gain the *intellectual* initiative over the other party, and that is vitally important in the power game. The Democrats seized the "idea advantage" at the time of Franklin Roosevelt's New Deal; the Reagan Republicans seized it in the early 1980s with their idea of cutting government and taxes.
—*Hedrick Smith*, The Power Game: How Washington Works, *p. xvi*

The real pros . . . usually have a pretty good feel for how certain policy lines and maneuvers will play out, before they start.
—*Hedrick Smith*, The Power Game: How Washington Works, *p. xvii*

The wise cabinet secretary knows you build a partnership with the chairmen of the Congressional committees that watch over your department, even if they come from the opposite party.
—*Hedrick Smith*, The Power Game: How Washington Works, *p. xviii*

Command is less effective than consensus.
—*Hedrick Smith*, The Power Game: How Washington Works, *p. xx*

Power is the ability to make something happen or to keep it from happening.
—*Hedrick Smith*, The Power Game: How Washington Works, *p. xxi*

Some politicians have played the power game well and largely gotten their way, and others have played it badly and seen their policies falter.
—*Hedrick Smith*, The Power Game: How Washington Works, *p. xxi*

In Washington, as elsewhere, power does not always follow organizational charts; a person's title does not necessarily reflect the power that he or she has.
—*Hedrick Smith*, The Power Game: How Washington Works, *p. xxii*

We have to be willing to step outside of our comfort zone, or be shoved out of our comfort zones, before we usually look around for new solutions.
—*Blaine Lee*, The Power Principle, *p. 185*

The best leader is rarely the best pitcher or catcher. The best leader is just what's advertised: the best leader. Leaders get their kicks from orchestrating the work of others—not from doing it themselves.
—*Tom Peters*, Fast Company, *2001*

Today, a leader must act as a tension thermostat, responsible for keeping tension at optimum levels and making adjustments when the level is too high or too low.
—*Victor Buzzotta*, Making Common Sense Common Practice

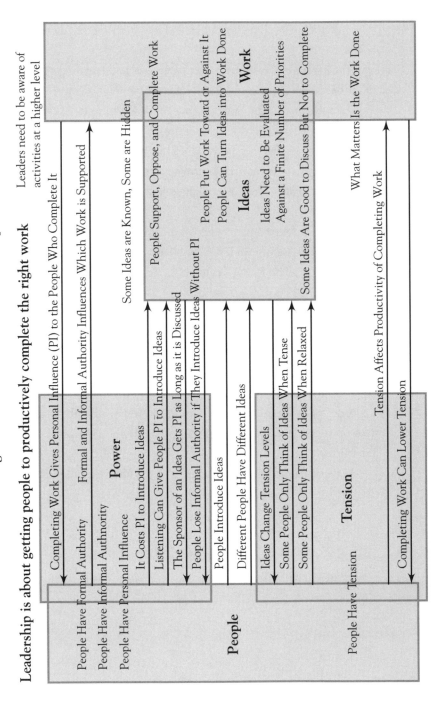

Figure A.1 A Structure for Leadership

Leadership is about getting people to productively complete the right work

Organized Leadership Content

Goal of Leadership

The goal of leadership is to complete the right work and prevent from being completed the wrong work.

Had Roosevelt and Churchill not rallied the Western democracies, civilization might have perished.
> —*David R. Gergen*, Eyewitness to Power:
> The Essence of Leadership, Nixon to Clinton, *p. 12*

In the movie *The Candidate*, Robert Redford wins election and famously asks, "What do we do now?"
> —*David R. Gergen*, Eyewitness to Power:
> The Essence of Leadership, Nixon to Clinton, *p. 171*

Power is the ability to make something happen or to keep it from happening.
> —*Hedrick Smith*, The Power Game: How Washington Works, *p. xxi*

York divided people into two categories: those who got the job done and those who didn't.
> —*Doug Garr*, IBM Redux: Lou Gerstner and
> the Business Turnaround of the Decade, *p. 51*

How do we go about changing a culture that involves thousands of people, most of whom, from a distance, seem quite satisfied with things the way they are?
> —*Peter Block,* The Empowered Manager:
> Positive Political Skills at Work, *p. xvii*

IBM wanted a capable businessman with fresh ideas.
    —*Doug Garr*, IBM Redux: Lou Gerstner and
        the Business Turnaround of the Decade, *p. 25*

The boss may have the power to fire workers and injure the worker's record,
but the boss, by the imposition of power, can never force his employee to
work to his capacity or to create.
    —*Gerry L. Spence*, How to Argue and Win Every Time:
        At Home, at Work, in Court, Everywhere, Every Day, *p. 42*

Some politicians have played the power game well and largely gotten their
way, and others have played it badly and seen their policies falter.
    —*Hedrick Smith*, The Power Game: How Washington Works, *p. xxi*

I was really looking for people who were filled with passion and a desire to
get things done.
    —*Jack Welch*, Jack: Straight from the Gut, *p. 54*

[The intellectuals] often turned out to be unfocused dabblers, unwilling to
commit, lacking intensity and passion for any one thing.
    —*Jack Welch*, Jack: Straight from the Gut, *p. 54*

One of the shortcomings of American corporations is that they have focused
far too much on good strategy and not nearly enough on good implementation.
    —*David T. Kearns*, Prophets in the Dark: How Xerox
        Reinvented Itself and Beat Back the Japanese, *p. 278*

People there compete, take sides, form teams, and when one action is
finished, members form new sides for the next issue.
    —*Hedrick Smith*, The Power Game: How Washington Works, *p. xvi*

See simplicity in the complicated.
    —*Lao Tsu*, Tao Te Ching, *translated by*
        Gia-Fu Feng Jane English, and Gis-Fu Feng, Section 63

Leadership is action, not position.
—*Donald H. McGannon*

People can be leaders no matter where they are. Leadership is not about a
title, degree or level. Anybody can lead at any time.
—*Carly Fiorina, CEO of Hewlett-Packard*

The main reasons CEOs fail is not mistakes in strategy or finance but simple
inability to execute—to get done what they wanted to get done.
—*Geoffery Colvin*, Fortune, *December 10, 2001*

Even direct subordinates may resist your orders when they are convinced
you are wrong and will certainly drag their heels if they are afraid of proposed
changes. . . . Fewer and fewer decisions can be made or implemented in
isolation in the modern business organization.
—*Eliza G.C. Collins and Mary Anne Devanna,*
The New Portable MBA, *p. 33*

If I had eight hours to chop down a tree, I'd spend six sharpening my ax.
—*Abraham Lincoln*

We have become focused not on how to identify our own uniqueness, but
on how to mimic the mark and style of others. We have been told that if we
can look like others, act like others, indeed, argue as others, perhaps then we
can be successful. . . . The great quest is to find the individual "soul-print,"
the singular stamp that belongs only to us.
—*Gerry L. Spence*, How to Argue and Win Every Time:
At Home, at Work, in Court, Everywhere, Every Day, *p. 16*

With so much change and turbulence taking place, people need leaders
more than ever. Yet, with so many acquisitions, spin-offs, and launches
taking place, people insist on maintaining their independence more than
ever. And with so much decentralization and delayering of companies taking
place, people struggle even to know what leadership is more than ever.
—*The Founding Editors*, Fast Company, *1999*

Gerstner vowed to "seek to create brilliant strategies and execute them brilliantly."

> —*Doug Garr*, IBM Redux: Lou Gerstner and
> the Business Turnaround of the Decade, *p. 29*

Leaders Need to Be Aware of Activities at a Higher Level

The best leader is rarely the best pitcher or catcher. The best leader is just what's advertised: the best leader. Leaders get their kicks from orchestrating the work of others—not from doing it themselves.

> —*Tom Peters*, Fast Company, *2001*

The real pros . . . usually have a pretty good feel for how certain policy lines and maneuvers will play out, before they start.

> —*Hedrick Smith*, The Power Game: How Washington Works, *p. xvii*

Reagan was as good that day as he had ever been in meetings. He stayed above the forest of facts we had provided and focused on the larger goals he wanted to pursue.

> —*David R. Gergen*, Eyewitness to Power:
> The Essence of Leadership, Nixon to Clinton, *p. 153*

Gaining and Sharing Power

Power is nothing unless you can turn it into influence.

> —*Condoleeza Rice, quoted in* Readers' Digest, *November 2002*

All leadership is influence.

> —*John C. Maxwell, Injoy, Inc.*

No president can succeed unless he can build a governing coalition.

> —*Hedrick Smith*, The Power Game: How Washington Works, *p. 453*

To be a player is to have power or influence on some issue.

> —*Hedrick Smith*, The Power Game: How Washington Works, *p. xiii*

The wise cabinet secretary knows you build a partnership with the chairmen of the Congressional committees that watch over your department, even if they come from the opposite party.

> —*Hedrick Smith*, The Power Game: How Washington Works, *p. xviii*

Command is less effective than consensus.

> —*Hedrick Smith*, The Power Game: How Washington Works, *p. xx*

Demand commitment instead of sacrifice.

> —*Peter Block*, The Empowered Manager:
> Positive Political Skills at Work, *p. 75*

Rickard knew that if the quality program was going to get anyplace in the organization he would have to place on the support of the princes and to dance past the kings.

> —*David T. Kearns*, Prophets in the Dark: How Xerox
> Reinvented Itself and Beat Back the Japanese, *p. 172*

Formal Authority

Many in positions of power take up such posts in the fulfillment of a neurotic need to exercise power over others.

> —*Gerry L. Spence*, How to Argue and Win Every Time:
> At Home, at Work, in Court, Everywhere, Every Day, *p. 43*

Informal Authority

In Washington, as elsewhere, power does not always follow organizational charts; a person's title does not necessarily reflect the power that he or she has.

> —*Hedrick Smith*, The Power Game: How Washington Works, *p. xxii*

Jack Kennedy . . . was the first successful presidential candidate to rely on personal appeal . . . to win the top prize.

> —*Hedrick Smith*, The Power Game: How Washington Works, *p. 694*

The word "trust" appears in virtually every current book on leadership, and it is taken as a commonplace that without trust, leadership is impossible. . . ."

> —*Robert C. Solomon*

Horse-trading is the way the battle is fought in the final clinches.
  —Hedrick Smith, The Power Game: How Washington Works, *p. 477*

Personal Influence

The agenda game must be won first.
  —Hedrick Smith, The Power Game: How Washington Works, *p. 333*

Write up your idea in a memo. People may roll their eyes if you bring a written handout, but at least there won't be any doubt as to whose it is.
  —Sarah Myers McGinty, Ph.D., quoted by Anne Fisher, Fortune, *2001*

One political party, for example, can gain the intellectual initiative over the other party, and that is vitally important in the power game. The Democrats seized the "idea advantage" at the time of Franklin Roosevelt's New Deal; the Reagan Republicans seized it in the early 1980s with their idea of cutting government and taxes.
  —Hedrick Smith, The Power Game: How Washington Works, *p. xvi*

Strike quickly for a win, during the early rush of power. That helps establish momentum and an aura of success.
  —Hedrick Smith, The Power Game: How Washington Works, *p. 456*

Winning is power.
  —Hedrick Smith, The Power Game: How Washington Works, *p. 456*

Generating Ideas

The best way to have a good idea is to have a lot of ideas.
  —Dr. Linus Pauling

Already intellectually drained and bankrupt of ideas, [IBM] was now leaderless and rudderless.
  —Doug Garr, IBM Redux: Lou Gerstner and
    the Business Turnaround of the Decade, *p. 20*

The creation of vision comes from a considerable amount of exploring, analyzing, and rooting around in the territory of the problem.
>—*Eliza G.C. Collins and Mary Anne Devanna,*
>The New Portable MBA, *p. 54*

Knowing ignorance is strength. Ignoring knowledge is sickness.
>—*Lao Tsu,* Tao Te Ching, *translated by*
>*Gia-Fu Feng Jane English, and Gis-Fu Feng, Section 71*

After spending nearly five years in Beirut, I eventually developed the imagination the city demanded.
>—*Thomas L. Friedman,* From Beirut to Jerusalem, *p. 23*

Nixon liked a diversity of voices on his staff.
>—*David R. Gergen,* Eyewitness to Power:
>The Essence of Leadership, Nixon to Clinton, *p. 23*

Bob. . . had a million ideas and brought new life to the position.
>—*Jack Welch,* Jack: Straight from the Gut, *p. 47*

Listening Can Give Enough Power to People to Introduce Their Ideas

It was refreshing to many IBMers that Gerstner actually read their messages.
>—*Doug Garr,* IBM Redux: Lou Gerstner and
>the Business Turnaround of the Decade, *p. 35*

Sometimes those who refuse to cooperate actually have valuable knowledge or abilities; they may even be indispensable to your success.
>—*Eliza G.C. Collins and Mary Anne Devanna,*
>The New Portable MBA, *p. 33*

Gerstner did a lot of listening, not just to customers, but to the legions of analysts and technology pundits.
>—*Doug Garr,* IBM Redux: Lou Gerstner and
>the Business Turnaround of the Decade, *p. 59*

If I were required to choose the single essential skill from the many that make up the art of the argument, it would be the ability to listen.

> —*Gerry L. Spence*, How to Argue and Win Every Time:
> At Home, at Work, in Court, Everywhere, Every Day, *p. 67*

Some People Think of Ideas when They Are Relaxed, Some when They Are Tense

Most creativity comes at one of two times: When your back is against the wall or in a time of calm.

> —*Rusty Rueff, Senior Vice President of Human Resources,*
> *Electronic Arts, Rusty Rueff,* Fortune, *January 20, 2003, p. 152*

We have to be willing to step outside of our comfort zone, or be shoved out of our comfort zones, before we usually look around for new solutions.

> —*Blaine Lee*, The Power Principle, *p. 185*

There is nothing like the sight of the gallows to clear the mind.

> —*Gary Tooker, Motorola, Inc.*

The mind can be programmed to help solve problems, to enhance insight, intuition, and inspiration. All you have to do to access this part of your brain is to relax. Don't force creativity, coax it. Mindless activities like exercise, driving, and even watching television are great idea generators. Many people get their best ideas in the shower or just as they fall asleep. The key is to get into the right state of mind—the state of relaxation.

> —*Barry Goldsmith, CEO, Goldsmith Consulting,*
> *quoted in* Los Angeles Business Journal, *August 28, 2001*

In a newspaper interview, Paul McCartney described how he wrote the song "Yellow Submarine" when relaxed in bed just before dropping off to sleep.

> —*Quoted in the Creation Foundation*

You're always more creative when relaxed.

> —*Lighthousewriters.com*

Moderating a Productive Tension

Today, a leader must act as a tension thermostat, responsible for keeping tension at optimum levels and making adjustments when the level is too high or too low.

— *Victor Buzzotta*, Making Common Sense Common Practice

When times are good you should talk about what needs improvement, and when things are bad you should assure people they will get better.

— *Anne Mulcahy, Chair and CEO, Xerox Corporation,*
at the Executive's Club of Chicago, March 14, 2002

Fear is painful. I hate its frequent companionship. Yet it challenges me. It energizes my senses.

— *Gerry L. Spence*, How to Argue and Win Every Time:
At Home, at Work, in Court, Everywhere, Every Day, *p. 14*

Strategic intent aims to create employee excitement, not just employee satisfaction. The more excited a worker is, the less are remuneration and hygiene the sole barometer of contentment.

— *Gary Hamel and C.K. Prahalad*, Competing for the Future, *p. 135*

Gerstner tried to shake up AMEX managers.

— *Doug Garr*, IBM Redux: Lou Gerstner and the Business
Turnaround of the Decade, *p. 96*

You can't wait around until everyone feels pain from the marketplace, because then it's too late. So you need to use some induced pain. You have to throw a few punches here and there.

— *David T. Kearns*, Prophets in the Dark: How Xerox
Reinvented Itself and Beat Back the Japanese, *p. 280*

Anyone can become angry—that is easy. But to be angry with the right person, to the right degree, at the right time, for the right purpose, and in the right way—that is not easy.

— *Aristotle*

Czarnecki was just a very nice guy, too nice for the new IBM.
> —*Doug Garr*, IBM Redux: Lou Gerstner and
> the Business Turnaround of the Decade, *p. 53*

Maybe if they threw a few swears around, they could jump-start some somnolent brains.
> —*Doug Garr*, IBM Redux: Lou Gerstner and
> the Business Turnaround of the Decade, *p. 45*

Bring humor into the workplace where possible. Laughing eases tension and stress and reduces anxiety levels. It also makes for a more personalized work atmosphere.
> —*Bob Adams*, The Everything Leadership

Completing the Right Work and Preventing the Wrong Work

A "deliverable" was a tangible short-term assignment with an inviolable deadline.
> —*Doug Garr*, IBM Redux: Lou Gerstner and
> the Business Turnaround of the Decade, *p. 97*

Ideas Need to Be Evaluated Against a Finite Number of Priorities

The capacity of any president to lead depends on focusing the nation's political attention and energies on two or three top priorities.
> —*Hedrick Smith*, The Power Game: How Washington Works, *p. 333*

People Are More Likely to Support an Idea They Introduced

If I participate in creating the change, I'm going to understand it better, and I am going to have ownership.
> —*David T. Kearns*, Prophets in the Dark: How Xerox
> Reinvented Itself and Beat Back the Japanese, *p. 280*

The patriarchal belief is that self-restraint is essential to building a strong organization. . . . The price we pay for this attitude is that we put a cap on the well of people's motivation and passion and caring.

—*Peter Block*, The Empowered Manager:
Positive Political Skills at Work, *p. 71*

Index

About the Author

Clark Aldrich recently led the international team that created SimuLearn's Virtual Leader, which has been featured on CNN, *The New York Times*, and *U.S News and World Report*, and sold to some of the largest enterprises in the United States. Virtual Leader is currently being translated into other languages, and SimuLearn became an Eduventures 100 company in 2003.

Mr. Aldrich speaks to, consults with, and writes for implementing enterprises, suppliers, and numerous publications, conferences, and venture capitalists about e-learning issues. He writes the popular monthly Industry Watch column for *Training* magazine.

In February 2002, Mr. Aldrich was listed as one of the twenty people to watch in the Lifelong Learning Market Report. In 2001, the American Society for Training and Development identified him as one of nine members of "training's new guard." In 2000, he was chosen as one of three e-learning "gurus" by *Fortune* magazine and was named one of *Training* magazine's sixteen visionaries of the industry.

Mr. Aldrich co-developed, chairs, and keynotes the e-Learning Supplier Summit, co-located with the annual Online Learning Conference.

While at Gartner Group, he was the research director responsible for creating and building their e-learning practice, where he developed strategies with Global 1000 organizations, vendors, and venture capitalists.

Prior to joining Gartner, he worked for nearly eight years at Xerox, where his responsibilities included special projects for the executive office. Mr. Aldrich earned a bachelor's degree in artificial intelligence and cognitive science from Brown University.

Pfeiffer Publications Guide

This guide is designed to familiarize you with the various types of Pfeiffer publications. The formats section describes the various types of products that we publish; the methodologies section describes the many different ways that content might be provided within a product. We also provide a list of the topic areas in which we publish.

FORMATS

In addition to its extensive book-publishing program, Pfeiffer offers content in an array of formats, from fieldbooks for the practitioner to complete, ready-to-use training packages that support group learning.

FIELDBOOK Designed to provide information and guidance to practitioners in the midst of action. Most fieldbooks are companions to another, sometimes earlier, work, from which its ideas are derived; the fieldbook makes practical what was theoretical in the original text. Fieldbooks can certainly be read from cover to cover. More likely, though, you'll find yourself bouncing around following a particular theme, or dipping in as the mood, and the situation, dictate.

HANDBOOK A contributed volume of work on a single topic, comprising an eclectic mix of ideas, case studies, and best practices sourced by practitioners and experts in the field.

An editor or team of editors usually is appointed to seek out contributors and to evaluate content for relevance to the topic. Think of a handbook not as a ready-to-eat meal, but as a cookbook of ingredients that enables you to create the most fitting experience for the occasion.

RESOURCE Materials designed to support group learning. They come in many forms: a complete, ready-to-use exercise (such as a game); a comprehensive resource on one topic (such as conflict management) containing a variety of methods and approaches; or a collection of like-minded activities (such as icebreakers) on multiple subjects and situations.

TRAINING PACKAGE An entire, ready-to-use learning program that focuses on a particular topic or skill. All packages comprise a guide for the facilitator/trainer and a workbook for the participants. Some packages are supported with additional media—such as video—or learning aids, instruments, or other devices to help participants understand concepts or practice and develop skills.

- *Facilitator/trainer's guide* Contains an introduction to the program, advice on how to organize and facilitate the learning event, and step-by-step instructor notes. The guide also contains copies of presentation materials—handouts, presentations, and overhead designs, for example—used in the program.

- *Participant's workbook* Contains exercises and reading materials that support the learning goal and serves as a valuable reference and support guide for participants in the weeks and months that follow the learning event. Typically, each participant will require his or her own workbook.

ELECTRONIC CD-ROMs and web-based products transform static Pfeiffer content into dynamic, interactive experiences. Designed to take advantage of the searchability, automation, and ease-of-use that technology provides, our e-products bring convenience and immediate accessibility to your workspace.

METHODOLOGIES

CASE STUDY A presentation, in narrative form, of an actual event that has occurred inside an organization. Case studies are not prescriptive, nor are they used to prove a point; they are designed to develop critical analysis and decision-making skills. A case study has a specific time frame, specifies a sequence of events, is narrative in structure, and contains a plot structure—an issue (what should be/have been done?). Use case studies when the goal is to enable participants to apply previously learned theories to the circumstances in the case, decide what is pertinent, identify the real issues, decide what should have been done, and develop a plan of action.

ENERGIZER A short activity that develops readiness for the next session or learning event. Energizers are most commonly used after a break or lunch to stimulate or refocus the group. Many involve some form of physical activity, so they are a useful way to counter post-lunch lethargy. Other uses include transitioning from one topic to another, where "mental" distancing is important.

EXPERIENTIAL LEARNING ACTIVITY (ELA) A facilitator-led intervention that moves participants through the learning cycle from experience to application (also known as a Structured Experience). ELAs are carefully thought-out designs in which there is a definite learning purpose and intended outcome. Each step—everything that participants do during the activity—facilitates the accomplishment of the stated goal. Each ELA includes complete instructions for facilitating the intervention and a clear statement of goals, suggested group size and timing, materials required, an explanation of the process, and, where appropriate, possible variations to the activity. (For more detail on Experiential Learning Activities, see the Introduction to the *Reference Guide to Handbooks and Annuals*, 1999 edition, Pfeiffer, San Francisco.)

GAME A group activity that has the purpose of fostering team spirit and togetherness in addition to the achievement of a pre-stated goal. Usually contrived—undertaking a desert expedition, for example—this type of learning method offers an engaging means for participants to demonstrate and practice business and interpersonal skills. Games are effective for team building and personal development mainly because the goal is subordinate to the process—the means through which participants reach decisions, collaborate, communicate, and generate trust and understanding. Games often engage teams in "friendly" competition.

ICEBREAKER A (usually) short activity designed to help participants overcome initial anxiety in a training session and/or to acquaint the participants with one another. An icebreaker can be a fun activity or can be tied to specific topics or training goals. While a useful tool in itself, the icebreaker comes into its own in situations where tension or resistance exists within a group.

INSTRUMENT A device used to assess, appraise, evaluate, describe, classify, and summarize various aspects of human behavior. The term used to describe an instrument depends primarily on its format and purpose. These terms include survey, questionnaire, inventory, diagnostic survey, and poll. Some uses of instruments include providing instrumental feedback to group members, studying here-and-now processes or functioning within a group, manipulating group composition, and evaluating outcomes of training and other interventions.

Instruments are popular in the training and HR field because, in general, more growth can occur if an individual is provided with a method for focusing specifically on his or her own behavior. Instruments also are used to obtain information that will serve as a basis for change and to assist in workforce planning efforts.

Paper-and-pencil tests still dominate the instrument landscape with a typical package comprising a facilitator's guide, which offers advice on administering the instrument and interpreting the collected data, and an initial set of instruments. Additional instruments are available separately. Pfeiffer, though, is investing heavily in e-instruments. Electronic instrumentation provides effortless distribution and, for larger groups particularly, offers advantages over paper-and-pencil tests in the time it takes to analyze data and provide feedback.

LECTURETTE A short talk that provides an explanation of a principle, model, or process that is pertinent to the participants' current learning needs. A lecturette is intended to establish a common language bond between the trainer and the participants by providing a mutual frame of reference. Use a lecturette as an introduction to a group activity or event, as an interjection during an event, or as a handout.

MODEL A graphic depiction of a system or process and the relationship among its elements. Models provide a frame of reference and something more tangible, and more easily remembered, than a verbal explanation. They also give participants something to "go on," enabling them to track their own progress as they experience the dynamics, processes, and relationships being depicted in the model.

ROLE PLAY A technique in which people assume a role in a situation/ scenario: a customer service rep in an angry-customer exchange, for example. The way in which the role is approached is then discussed and feedback is offered. The role play is often repeated using a different approach and/or incorporating changes made based on feedback received. In other words, role playing is a spontaneous interaction involving realistic behavior under artificial (and safe) conditions.

SIMULATION A methodology for understanding the interrelationships among components of a system or process. Simulations differ from games in that they test or use a model that depicts or mirrors some aspect of reality in form, if not necessarily in content. Learning occurs by studying the effects of change on one or more factors of the model. Simulations are commonly used to test hypotheses about what happens in a system—often referred to as "what if?" analysis—or to examine best-case/worst-case scenarios.

THEORY A presentation of an idea from a conjectural perspective. Theories are useful because they encourage us to examine behavior and phenomena through a different lens.

TOPICS

The twin goals of providing effective and practical solutions for workforce training and organization development and meeting the educational needs of training and human resource professionals shape Pfeiffer's publishing program. Core topics include the following:

Leadership and Management

Communication and Presentation

Coaching and Mentoring

Training and Development

e-Learning

Teams and Collaboration

OD and Strategic Planning

Human Resources

Consulting